STUDY GUIDE

Volume I

to accompany

Kishlansky   Geary   O'Brien

CIVILIZATION IN THE WEST

Third Edition

John Paul Bischoff

Oklahoma State University

 **LONGMAN**

An Imprint of Addison Wesley Longman, Inc.

New York • Reading, Massachusetts • Menlo Park, California • Harlow, England
Don Mills, Ontario • Sydney • Mexico City • Madrid • Amsterdam

Study Guide to accompany Kishlansky, Geary, O'Brien, *Civilization in the West*, Third Edition, Volume I.

Copyright © 1998 Longman Publishers USA, a division of Addison Wesley Longman, Inc.

ISBN: 0-321-01639-4

CB

99 00 01 02 9 8 7 6 5 4 3 2

CONTENTS

Introduction

The *Study Guide* is keyed to help the student understand the comparative and connective aspects of the text. Rather than focus on rote memorization of data, the *Study Guide* emphasizes recognition of major themes and interpretation of connective links among civilizations. Each chapter within the text is covered in the *Study Guide* so that the student proceeds from the specific data to the important summary themes and comparative conclusions.

Most chapters of the *Study Guide* include the following elements:

- An outline demonstrating the organization of each chapter in the text and the major historical points covered;

- A timeline asking the student to organize major events in each chapter chronologically;

- A list of important terms, people, and events to be defined;

- A map exercise establishing the geopolitical structure of the chapter;

- A series of short questions entitled "Making Connections" seeking to establish students' familiarity with larger blocks of information connecting the items found in "Terms, People, Events;"

- Two broad essays stressing the major interpretive points of each chapter and asking students to make significant comparisons and contrasts among historical periods;

- A self-test of factual information featuring multiple-choice questions covering both specific data and general interpretations. A selection of these questions is taken directly from the *Test Bank* for *Civilization in the West*.

How should you use the *Study Guide*? Read the text chapter first. The *Study Guide* was not intended to replace the text, simply to supplement it. After your first reading, look at the outline in the *Study Guide*. The outline should help you to organize the elements of the chapter and point out important concepts. Arrange the chapter chronologically by filling out the timeline. It may be helpful to compare the timeline for the chapter on which you are working with those of other chapters to gain a comparative view of political, social, and economic events. Once the organization of the chapter and its chronological framework is clear to you, move on to the "Terms, People, Events." These specific points of information can best be handled by writing out definitions for each—perhaps in your notebook. You may discover that these terms can be supplemented by items covered in lecture. "Making Connections" asks you to take the major points in the outline and put them together in short essay form. The purpose of putting blocks of information together is to make certain that you understand relationships between important people and events. The last activity in the *Study Guide*, "Putting Larger Concepts Together", asks you to make broad generalizations about the major themes of each chapter and, occasionally, to compare the ideas explored in one chapter with material from earlier chapters. These may be more difficult to accomplish, but they check your ability to understand the comparative developments in European history. Essays covered in "Putting Larger Concepts Together" could be used as a focus for in-class discussion or possibly as examination questions. Remember, the *Study Guide* is coordinated with the *Test Bank*.

No study guide can guarantee a good grade. The text and the *Study Guide* represent only one component of the course. Individual instructors may vary in their approaches to the course. Lectures may incorporate materials not included in the text or differ dramatically in interpretation. Instructors may opt not to use the *Test Bank* in order to offer questions that more closely parallel their own treatment of the course. In any case, the *Study Guide* will strengthen your understanding of *Civilization in the West* and enable you to understand the broad patterns of change in European history.

Chapter 1

The First Civilizations

OUTLINE

I.   The Idea of Civilization

The West is an idea that developed slowly during Greek and Roman civilization. Initially the Greeks referred to their homeland as the "West." The Romans took up the concept and applied it to the western half of their empire. Asia—or the East—was similarly a geographical innovation of the Greeks and Romans. Asia was that land that belonged to non-Greek cultures of Asia Minor, particularly the Persians. The Romans, too, regarded lands east of Greece as Asia. The name was retained and applied to other cultures beyond the Turkish peninsula such as China and India. Although what we refer to as "Western Civilization" began in the area that today we call the Middle East, we tend to associate the term more with developments in Europe, particularly after the birth of Christ. After the sixteenth century, Western civilization was exported through the process of conquest and colonization beyond the confines of Europe throughout the world. The exportation of Western civilization superimposed western culture on ancient traditions of art, science, economy, and politics in Asia, Africa, and the New World. The results of the exportation of Western civilization have been mixed. Both positive and negative results have emerged along with a new global culture.

II.   Before Civilization

The first pre-humans appeared as early as five million years ago. They were toolmakers and survived by hunting and gathering. The first immediate ancestors of man, *Homo sapiens*, appeared over a hundred thousand years ago. One of the earliest varieties of *Homo sapiens* was Neanderthal man. Although closely related in structure and culture to modern man, Neanderthal man mysteriously disappeared about forty thousand years ago. Our immediate ancestors were *Homo sapiens sapiens*. All current races are descended from this subspecies. Early varieties of *Homo sapiens sapiens* lived as small bands of hunter-gatherers. Their original material culture consisted of the production of stone and bone tools. By the late Paleolithic period (35,000–10,000 B.C.), early humans had produced art and appear to have formulated religious practices related to fertility and fecundity in the natural world around them. Around 10,000 B.C., hunter-gatherers residing in the Middle East began to become more sedentary. They stopped following the herds of wild animals and began to exploit the resources of a single area more completely. The transition to sedentary communities was most prominent along the shores of the Mediterranean and the foothills of the Zagros Mountains. Sedentary life permitted more rapid population growth and created a demand for greater food supplies. The demand for a more intense exploitation of the environment led to domestication of animals and cereal agriculture. Sedentary agricultural societies required more formal political organization in order to exploit the environment effectively. Religious rites of various types also became more important in agricultural societies.

III.   Mesopotamia: Between the Two Rivers

A.   The Ramparts of Uruk

Mesopotamia was not naturally well suited to agriculture. Only the southern portions of the land between the Tigris and Euphrates—the area called Sumeria—were fertile, and limited rainfall necessitated irrigation. In order to make use of the river plains, villages concentrated into larger urban centers. Urban development became pronounced around 3000 B.C. The cities of Mesopotamia produced new social, political, and cultural systems. Religious priesthoods and military leaders created political and social elites. Beneath the elites were slaves, peasants who worked the land belonging to the elites, skilled workers who served the temple complexes, and free landowners. The Mesopotamian city-state also contained a large number of slave women who served as laborers in the textile industries. Although the overall status of free women was somewhat better, the Mesopotamian city-state established the male dominance pattern in households. Mesopotamian city-states allowed economic specialization and technological advance.   Innovations were made in irrigation, transportation on land and sea, pottery, and metalworking. Writing was also developed in Mesopotamia.   Writing permitted greater centralization and control, enabled communication throughout the administrative units, allowed the management of commerce, and recorded the achievements of the political elites.

B.   Gods and Mortals in Mesopotamia

Polytheism was the rule in Mesopotamia. The gods were anthropomorphic—they looked and acted like people. There were both greater and lesser gods. The greatest divinities were those of the sky, air, and rivers. Temple complexes dominated both the landscape and the economy of Mesopotamian city-states. Although the people sought a positive relationship with the gods through special rituals and donations in order to secure their protection and aid in this world, Mesopotamian religion did not offer hope of an afterlife.

C.   Sargon and Mesopotamian Expansion

Mesopotamia was divided into warring city-states until about 2300 B.C. The first ruler to unify the southern portion of Mesopotamia was Sargon of Akkad. Sargon conquered the other major cities and appointed his officials to govern them. He also broke the power of the local temple complexes by redistributing their lands and wealth among his followers. Sargon's unification of Sumeria was a temporary accomplishment of a brilliant commander and ruler. His empire did not long survive him.

D.   Hammurabi and the Old Babylonian Empire

With the fall of Sargon's unified Sumerian state, political dominance passed farther to the north, to the middle region of Mesopotamia. By 1750 B.C. the city of Babylon exerted its influence over all the city-states between the rivers. The greatest ruler of Old Babylonia was Hammurabi, who is most famous for his strict code of laws imposed on all the city-states of his empire. The laws covered all aspects of Babylonian life: commerce, agriculture, marriage, crime, professional licensing, and domestic tranquility. Babylonian mathematicians also made significant advances in science and technology. Like Sargon before him, Hammurabi was unable to construct a lasting political unification of Mesopotamia. By 1600 B.C. the Babylonian Empire fell to foreign invaders, the Hittites from Anatolia. The Indo-European Hittite state emerged in Anatolia under the cultural influence of Mesopotamian civilization. The state expanded on the basis of political centralization, iron metallurgy, and the use of the war chariot. The Hittites destroyed the Babyonian state around 1600 B.C. and continued to expand southward until they came in contact with Egyptian civilization.

IV.   The Gift of the Nile

A.   Tending the Cattle of God

The Nile River valley that gave rise to Egyptian civilization was capable of supporting a dense population. Unlike Mesopotamia, the Nile ecology was more easily converted to sedentary agriculture and required little human intervention to produce crops. The Nile valley was also protected along its length by deserts; thus its agricultural settlements did not require walls for defense. Agricultural villages first appeared in the Nile valley about 4000 B.C. The agricultural communities were at first divided politically into two halves: northern or Lower Egypt near the Nile delta and southern or Upper Egypt. Around 3150 B.C. the ruler or pharaoh of Upper Egypt, Narmer, united the two halves and established a single capital at Memphis. Old Kingdom Egypt lasted from around 2770–2200 B.C. The king or pharaoh was a living god who was responsible for the flooding of the Nile and the preservation of *maat*, the harmony of the universe. Old Kingdom Egypt, defended by its surrounding deserts, was less militarized than Mesopotamia. The royal administration was peopled by priests and trained bureaucrats that governed agriculture, allocated labor to public works, and managed the organization of trade. Local governors administered local districts called *nomes*. Most important in the religious life of the Old Kingdom were the cults of the dead pharaohs. King Zoser, the first ruler of the Old Kingdom, began the practice of building pyramids surrounded by temples to serve the spirits of departed rulers. The first pyramids were built at Sakkara. These burial complexes became the focus of public works and labor. Eventually, the practice of creating shrines to the dead spread beyond the royal family to other members of the royal administration and then gradually to all men who could afford the costs of embalming and burial. Temple priesthoods and religious foundations devoted to cults of the dead began to receive greater and greater amounts of land and wealth to support their devotion to the departed spirits. By 2200 B.C. the temple priesthoods rivaled the kings in wealth and control of land. The unified Old Kingdom fragmented and royal authority disappeared. Provincial governors exercised political authority for nearly two hundred years.

B.   Democratization of the Afterlife

The governor of Thebes, a city in Upper Egypt, restored the unified government and established the Middle Kingdom of Egypt (around 2050–1786 B.C.). There was less distance between the elites and the common population in the Middle Kingdom. Burial complexes continued to be built, but without the magnificence that had typified the pyramids of the Old Kingdom. The administration was opened to all men of talent, including men born outside of Egypt. Foreign invaders from Palestine, the Hyksos, brought the Middle Kingdom to a close, although the foreign rulers adopted the customs of the defeated Egyptians. The Hyksos were also responsible for bringing new military technology—the war chariot and new bronze swords—into Egypt.

C.   The Egyptian Empire

The Theban rule Ahmose I expelled the Hyksos and initiated the New Kingdom (around 1560–1087 B.C.). The rulers of the New Kingdom extended Egyptian control beyond the Nile valley for the first time. Under Thutmose I (1506–1494 B.C.), Egyptian authority ran from Nubia in the south to the borders of Mesopotamia in the north. The expanded frontiers of Egypt brought the Nile valley civilization into contact with the other civilizations of the Middle East and the Mediterranean. Egyptian politics was often a precarious balance between the kings and the priesthoods of the religious cults. During the New Kingdom, King Amenhotep IV (1364–1347 B.C.) attempted to curtail the authority of the traditional religious cults by creating a new deity, the sun-disk god Aten. Amenhotep moved to a new capital dedicated to Aten and changed his name to Akhenaten in honor of the new god. The radical religious reform did not outlive Akhenaten. The next pharaoh, Tutankhamen, restored the traditional cults and festivals. With the restoration of the ancient religion came the return of the political struggle between the kings and the priesthoods. King Ramses II (1289–1224 B.C.) temporarily stopped the advance of the Hittites into Egypt, but the New Kingdom disintegrated shortly thereafter. The internal collapse of the Egyptians was mirrored in the fall of other centers of civilization at the same time.

V.   Between Two Worlds

A.   A Hebrew Alternative

Not all ancient peoples were organized in well-developed cultures such as Mesopotamia and Egypt. There were many nomadic herdsmen who existed on the fringes of civilizations. The Book of Genesis describes the wanderings of one of these Aramaean nomadic tribes, the family of the patriarch Abraham. Originally from the city-state of Ur, Abraham's tribe carried a mixed culture of Mesopotamian and nomadic origins. The clan was patriarchal in structure, and women played a subordinate role. The group worshipped a single deity peculiar to the clan, although they recognized the existence of other gods. Descendants of Abraham's clan entered Egypt in the period of disorder and foreign invasion at the end of the Middle Kingdom. They were probably reduced to slavery after the expulsion of the Hyksos and the establishment of the New Kingdom. During the decline of the New Kingdom, the descendants of the original clan left Egypt under the leadership of Moses. During the years of migration and the subsequent conquest of Palestine, the contacts with other cultures modified the political structure and belief system of followers of Moses—now known as the tribes of Israel. They became strictly monotheistic and accepted the god Yahweh (whom they had adopted from a tribe in the Sinai desert). The Israelites also accepted a strict code of laws received from Moses.

B.   A King Like All the Nations

The Israelites succeeded in conquering Palestine at a time when both the Hittites and Egyptians were powerless to prevent their takeover of the disputed territory. While at first the Israelites remained a loose confederation of tribes, they were forced to consolidate under the threat of invasion by the neighboring Philistines. After an initial defeat, the religious leaders of the Israelites consented to the creation of a kingdom. The Kingdom of Israel reached its zenith under David (around 1000–961 B.C.) and Solomon (around 961–922 B.C.). Under these monarchs Jerusalem was established as the capital and religious center of Israel. Political unification led to royal tyranny, particularly under Solomon. In order to protect the sacred covenant with Yahweh, prophets criticized the kings, called for reform, and established a tradition of religious opposition to absolutism. The unification of Israel ended after the reign of Solomon with the division of the kingdom into two halves: the kingdom of Israel in the north with a new capital at Shechem, and the kingdom of Judah in the south with the traditional capital at Jerusalem. Both kingdoms fell to foreign invaders. The Assyrians captured Israel in 722 B.C., and the New Babylonian Empire conquered Judah in 586 B.C. The Babylonians carried

4

off many of the elite of Judah to Mesopotamia, where the captives restructured their understanding of the covenant and began to emphasize strict monotheism. When the captives returned to Judah from their years of exile, they brought with them a reconstructed Judaism that was particularly concerned to maintain religious purity uncontaminated by other beliefs. Two traditions emerged. The Pharisees produced a body of oral law, the Mishnah, that eventually became the Talmud. The Pharisees also taught that a messiah would emerge to restore the independence of the Hebrews. The more conservative Sadducees emphasized the traditional Torah.

VI.   Nineveh and Babylon

The civilization that overcame Old Babylonia, New Kingdom Egypt, and Israel was the Assyrians. The Assyrians tied together Mesopotamia, Palestine, and the Nile River valley. They successfully created a more unified and homogeneous empire than any of their predecessors. Assyria began as a small state without significant resources in northern Mesopotamia. After a revolt that threatened to destroy the early Assyrian state, Tiglath-pileser III (746-727 B.C.) began the construction of the Assyrian empire. Assyrian military success was based on a professional rather than a volunteer army. The Assyrian state god not only sanctioned but demanded military activity. Ruthless measures consolidated conquests. Assyrian kings liquidated the elites of conquered territories, transported populations from one conquered territory to another to break down regional identities, and carried out campaigns of terror against populations that resisted Assyrian advances. Despite the ferocity and thoroughness of Assyrian methods, the subject states of Media, Babylonia, and Egypt succeeded in destroying the Assyrian Empire in 612 B.C. The fall of Assyria led to the brief resuscitation of Babylonia in the central portion of Mesopotamia. The New Babylonian Empire reached its height under King Nebuchadnezzar II. The New Babylonian Empire fell to the Persians in 539 B.C.

TIMELINE

Insert the following events into the timeline. This should help you to compare important historical events chronologically.

beginning of Old Kingdom Egypt
end of Hammurabi's reign in Old Babylon
beginning of civilization

Sargon's reign in Sumeria
David's reign in Israel
beginning of New Kingdom Egypt

— 3500 B.C.

— 2770 B.C.

— 2334-2279 B.C.

— 1750 B.C.

— 1560 B.C.

— 1000-961 B.C.

TERMS, PEOPLE, EVENTS

The following terms, people, and events are important to your understanding of the chapter. Define each one.

civilization
Mesopotamia
Epic of Gilgamesh
Sargon of Akkad
Babylon
Middle Kingdom
Hyksos
Hebrews
David
Talmud
Tiglath-pileser III

Homo sapiens
Sumer
cuneiform
Code of Hammurabi
pharaoh
New Kingdom
Ahmose
Abraham
prophets
Pharisees

Neanderthal
ziggurat
Uruk
Hittites
Old Kingdom
pyramids
Akhenaten
Yahweh
Torah
Assyria

MAP EXERCISE

The following exercise is intended to clarify the geophysical environment and the spatial relationships among the important objects and places mentioned in the chapter. Locate the following places on the map.

Tigris and Euphrates Rivers   Nile River
Sumer   Babylon
Memphis   Thebes

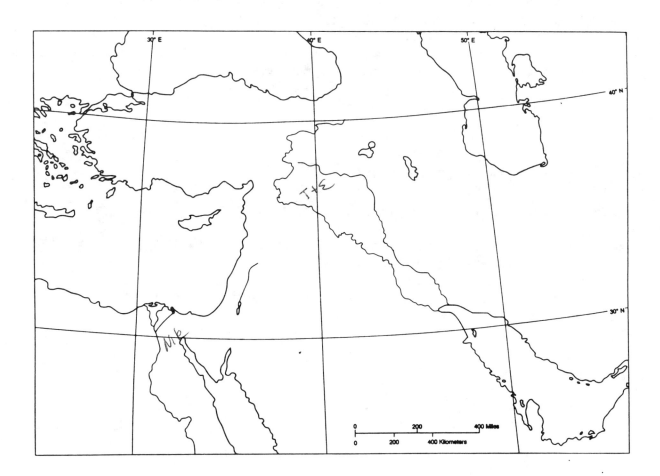

1.   How critical were river systems to the early civilizations of the Middle East? Were there any exceptions? How do you explain them?

2.   Where did the outside invaders (Hittites, Hyksos) of the early civilizations originate? What does this suggest about the relationship between mountains, steppes, and river plains?

MAKING CONNECTIONS

The following questions are intended to emphasize important ideas within the chapter.

1. Why was the agricultural revolution of the Neolithic so important to the development of civilization? How was human society different after the Neolithic revolution?

2. Discuss the political and social organization of Mesopotamia. Why were early empires in Mesopotamia so brief?

3. Discuss the political and social organization of Egypt. Why did this provide such stability in Egyptian civilization? What caused the downfall of the Egyptian Empire?

4. Discuss the early political and social organization of the Hebrews. Why did they eventually develop kingship? What was the religious significance of the Hebrews?

5. How did the Assyrian Empire provide a "blueprint" for future imperial systems?

PUTTING LARGER CONCEPTS TOGETHER

The following questions test your ability to summarize the major conclusions of the chapter.

1. What developments were characteristic of all early civilizations? Can you develop your own definition of civilization based on the common characteristics?

2. Did Egyptian or Mesopotamian civilization reach the imperial stage of development first? How can you account for the difference between the two civilizations?

SELF-TEST OF FACTUAL INFORMATION

1. The first humanlike creatures, such as Lucy, may have originated as early as

   a. five million years ago.
   b. three million years ago.
   c. one hundred thousand years ago.
   d. ten thousand years ago.

2. The statement that the agricultural revolution was portable means that

   a. Neolithic society became less sedentary.
   b. agricultural sites had to be located near rivers.
   c. the knowledge and technology of agriculture could easily be transported from one place to another.
   d. agriculture was strictly dependent on the existence of wheeled vehicles.

3. The founder of the first great nation-state who was known as the lord of Sumer was

   a. Sargon.
   b. Shulgi.
   c. Menes.
   d. Hammurabi.

4. What led to the increase of urban population in Mesopotamia at the expense of the countryside?

   a. plague
   b. raids by nomadic tribesmen and residents of neighboring towns
   c. failure of the agricultural systems in the countryside
   d. the successful expansion of small agricultural villages at the expense of larger urban centers

5. One of the most striking features of Egyptian religion during the Old and Middle Kingdoms was

   a. the absence of a belief in the afterlife.
   b. monotheism.
   c. a priesthood composed almost entirely of women.
   d. temple/tomb complexes for dead kings.

6. It is *most* accurate to state that the early nomadic groups of Hebrews or Aramaeans

   a. were not strictly monotheistic.
   b. accepted all the Mesopotamian gods.
   c. identified two special gods for each clan.
   d. were greatly influenced by Akhenaten.

7. The Hebrews

    a. never established a united kingdom.
    b. remained part of the Egyptian empire, even after the exodus from Egypt.
    c. were divided into two kingdoms, Israel and Judah, after Solomon's death.
    d. were able to establish an empire including Babylon and Nineveh.

8. After the Babylonian captivity of the people of Judah ended,

    a. a strongly centralized kingdom without the interference of prophets was established.
    b. Judaism ceased to exist as a meaningful religion.
    c. Ezra and Nehemiah revived piety by emphasizing the Torah and religious purity.
    d. the center of Judaism shifted from Israel to Persia.

9. What unique accomplishment did Assyrian civilization achieve?

    a. the unification of the Mesopotamian floodplain and Egypt
    b. the development of a writing system
    c. the establishment of cities as the basis for government
    d. the identification of the rulers with deities

10. Under what ruler did the New Babylonian Empire reach its zenith?

    a. Hammurabi
    b. Nebuchadnezzar II
    c. Tiglath-pileser III
    d. Sargon

Chapter 2

Early Greece, 2500 B.C.–500 B.C.

OUTLINE

I. Hecuba and Achilles

The Homeric epic poem, the *Iliad*, incorporates much of the fundamental psychology of early Greek society. Achilles is one of the central characters of the story and the ideal representation of Greek character. His search for revenge after the death of his friend, his physical victory over the champion of the Trojans, his humiliation of the enemy's corpse, and his pity for the parents of his vanquished opponent are symbolic of ideal Greek emotions in response to heroic situations.

II. Greece in the Bronze Age to 700 B.C.

A. Introduction

Homer's epic poems, the *Iliad* and the *Odyssey*, were written after the Bronze Age beginnings of Greece. The agricultural beginnings of Greek society date to ca. 3000 B.C. Unlike Mesopotamia and Egypt, Greece has few fertile plains. The land of Greece is divided into small ecological niches separated by mountains and sea. The geography of Greece kept the early agricultural villages distinct and independent. Greek agriculture was not as productive as that of the other early civilizations. In these circumstances, three distinct Bronze Age cultures developed: Cycladic, Minoan, and Mycenaean.

B. Islands of Peace

Cycladic culture appeared ca. 3000 B.C. on the islands of the Aegean Sea between Asia Minor and the Greek mainland. Cycladic culture was not urbanized. The culture was highly skilled in metalworking and had established trade routes to carry metal crafts throughout the Aegean. The culture declined ca. 1550 B.C. Minoan culture appeared on the island of Crete ca. 2500 B.C. Crete was at the crossroads of the ancient world and served as an exchange point for goods traded between Egypt, Mesopotamia, Asia Minor (the Hittites), and the Greek mainland. Like Cycladic culture, Minoan culture was neither urbanized nor militarized. At the center of the religious, economic, and political life of Minoan civilization were great temple/palace complexes, the largest of which was the palace of Knossos. From the palaces, priests and bureaucrats controlled the extensive system of collection and redistribution of goods that supported the elites. To permit the administrative organization of the economy, Minoan culture developed a form of writing called Linear A. The palace/temple also served as the ritual center for Minoan religious practices. Much remains unknown about Minoan religious practices. Female fertility figures seem to have played a large part and may have contributed to raising the overall social status of women in Minoan society. Other rituals involved bulls as male fertility figures. There are even frescoes of a unique form of bullfighting in which the participants vaulted over the backs of the charging animals. On a darker note, some aspects of Minoan religion seem to have required human sacrifice. Minoan culture came to an end ca. 1200 B.C. The causes of the decline are debatable. Both natural causes and a possible invasion from the mainland may have contributed to the downfall.

C.   Mainland of War

Mycenaean culture appeared on the Greek mainland ca. 1600 B.C. Unlike the other two Bronze Age cultures of Greece, Mycenaean culture developed both walled cities and extensive militarization of society. Mycenaean kings and a military elite, rather than a priesthood, controlled the political and economic life of mainland Greece. As a region within the Minoan trade network, the Mycenaeans adopted a form of Cretan writing that became known as Linear B.

D.   The Dark Age

Mycenaean culture began to decline ca. 1200 B.C. Rivalry and constant warfare among small city-states, overpopulation, failure of the commercial network, and the fragility of the agricultural system all may have contributed to the collapse. The decline of Mycenaean culture is contemporary with the general collapse of civilizations throughout the Middle East. With the downfall of Mycenaean culture, the kings and military elites typical of the small city-states disappeared. Greek culture entered a Dark Age that lasted from ca. 1200 to 800 B.C. During the Dark Age, population migrations were common, and new groups of people—the Dorians, Ionians, and Aeolians—mingled with the remnants of the original population. Greek culture was carried throughout the Aegean and to the shores of Asia Minor. The culture of the Dark Ages was more primitive than the preceding Bronze Age cultures. Written language was lost. Art became less proficient. The loss of commercial systems led to the adoption of iron in place of bronze and to a total absence of luxury products. The *Iliad* and the *Odyssey*, both composed during the Dark Ages, give hints of subtle changes in political structure. Petty kingship of small territories was the rule. The king's authority was due to his personal prowess rather than vested in the office. When absent, the military aristocrats attempted to usurp his authority. By the eighth century B.C., the military aristocracy sought to eliminate the petty kings.

III.   Archaic Greece, 700–500 B.C.

A.   Introduction

Between 800 and 500 B.C., a revolution in Greek culture took place. New political and social structures, artistic and intellectual traditions emerged. A significant population increase signaled the change in Greek culture. The greater population reduced the relative isolation of communities in the Dark Ages, placed new demands on the already overburdened agricultural system, and forced the development of more complex political systems to reorganize the economy of the Greek world.

B.   *Ethnos* and *Polis*

The *ethne* were large political units consisting of many agricultural villages and settlements united by a common religious temple or site. *Ethne* were governed by a small group of major landowners. The *polis* was a new form of political organization devised after the Dark Ages. The origins of *poleis* were fortified centers often built on hilltops and dedicated to specific gods. Marketplaces and settlements clustered around the *poleis*. After the population growth of the eighth century, these nodal points of settlement became towns. The towns were dominated by kings or a small group of wealthy landowners. The *poleis* controlled the surrounding agricultural hinterlands, and the farmers became citizens of the *poleis*. The *polis* may have been copied from the political organization of the Phoenicians. The Greeks definitely adopted the Phoenician writing system. Gradually political participation within the polis expanded due to the democratization of warfare. During the Bronze Age and the Dark Age, warfare was the prerogative of the military aristocracy who engaged in single, champion combat. In Archaic Greece, warfare passed to heavily armed infantry, the *hoplites*, who fought in close formations called *phalanges*. Service in the military brought political rights to the increasing number of warrior/citizens. Strictly aristocratic rule was undermined in the *poleis* and replaced by various new constitutions.

C.   Colonists and Tyrants

Colonization and the political institution of tyranny were two responses to the political turmoil of the seventh century B.C. Between the eleventh and eighth century B.C., the population growth spurred migrations of Greeks to the Aegean islands and the coastline of Asia Minor. While the first colonization efforts were directed to the east, by 750 B.C. Greeks began the process of establishing colonies in the western Mediterranean in southern Italy and Sicily. Colonists were often single males who left their homes because of political or social disabilities. Newly established colonies retained some cultural ties with the home governments, but were otherwise politically independent. Tyrants arose as political leaders to overthrow established aristocratic elites within the *poleis*. Often tyrants sprang from the military organization of the *phalanges*. Tyrants were regarded as reformers who extended the franchise, undertook public projects, and in some cases protected small farmers against the depredations of great landowners. Tyrants stood outside the normal constitutions of the *poleis*, although they did not always overthrow the original political structure. Tyrannies could seldom be sustained beyond a single generation, because the tyrant's position was dependent on his personal appeal rather than a constitutional office.

D.   Gender and Power

While the general political tendency in Archaic Greece was to broaden the political franchise within the *poleis*, the trend to democratization did not extend to women. The Greek household was patriarchal, and most women were denied a public political role. The prevalence of bisexuality in Greek culture tended to accentuate male dominance. The only women in Greece who enjoyed a public life were prostitutes.

E.   Gods and Mortals

Greek religion was polytheistic. Greek gods were peculiarly anthropomorphic and shared in the full range of human foibles. There were no priesthoods in Greek society comparable to those of Egypt or Mesopotamia. Ritual worship of the deities was often controlled by lay leaders. Temples were public buildings that reflected the wealth and prestige of the *polis* in which they stood. There were two religious sanctuaries that attracted the devotion of all Greeks. Olympia was honored as the main sanctuary of Zeus, the patriarch of the gods. Every four years all political affairs in Greece were put on hold so that athletes could compete in honor of Zeus at the Olympic games. The second Panhellenic religious site was at Delphi, the location of the shrine to Apollo. Although Delphi also held festivals devoted to athletic participation, the real popularity of the shrine was due to the location of the oracle there. The oracle received divine, if cryptic, messages from Apollo to all questions.

13

F.   Myth and Reason

One of the things that held the politically diverse Greek population together was a shared store of mythic stories. Some described political origins, others the basic causes of the natural universe. One of the most common sources for Greek mythology were the Homeric epics. So prominent did myth become as an aspect of Greek culture that the mythical traditions followed colonists as they moved about the Mediterranean. In curious contradiction to their fascination with myth, the Greeks also sought rational explanations for the world that surrounded them. The Greeks believed that the natural universe could be reduced to reason or laws of behavior. Some of the early Greek philosophers were Anaximander of Samos, Anaximenes of Miletus, Thales of Miletus, and Heraclitus of Ephesus. With some exceptions, Greek society embraced this variety of nonreligious and rational teaching.

G.   Art and the Individual

Greek art was at first derivative of Egyptian and Mesopotamian styles, but developed an innovative and identifiable style of its own by the eighth century B.C. Greek art concentrated on the human form and the traditional heroic myths. In the Archaic Age, Greek pottery painting passed from simple geometric forms to "black figure style", black silhouettes on red clay backgrounds. In sculpture, Greek artists passed from the *kouros*—a male nude copied from Egyptian models—to increasingly more ideal forms of the human body. Public buildings, particularly temples, gave opportunities to Greek sculptors to portray heroic legends in the new style.

IV.   A Tale of Three Cities

A.   Introduction

Various political forms were introduced into the Greek *poleis* by the end of the sixth century B.C. Three cities serve as examples of the types of political constitutions: Corinth, Sparta, and Athens.

B.   Wealthy Corinth

A single aristocratic clan, the Bacchiads, dominated Corinthian political life until the middle of the seventh century B.C. Confronted with social and economic problems associated with population increase, the clan was unable to respond effectively. As was common throughout Greece, the crisis was resolved by the overthrow of the Bacchiads and the establishment of a tyranny supported by those outside the Bacchiad clan. The tyrants were Cypselus (ca. 655–627 B.C.) and his son, Periander (ca. 627–586 B.C.). The tyrants fostered colonization, encouraged public works, and sought to shift the financial burden away from the small farmers. A new constitution was created to destroy the oligarchic hold of the Bacchiads. Cypselus divided all Corinthian citizens into eight fictive tribes and three geographical regions. Ten representatives from each tribe were selected as a council of eighty to advise the tyrant. Following the rule of Periander, the tyranny was ended. The new Corinthian constitution established a council of eight who also served in the old council of eighty. The council tended to be self-perpetuating, and government in Corinth remained the province of the few. Corinth is an example of an oligarchic *polis*.

C.   Martial Sparta

The basis of the Spartan constitution was military organization. The Spartan form of government emerged in the seventh century B.C. in response to crisis. In the midst of an attempt to take land from another city-state, the small farmers of a previously conquered territory, Messenia, rebelled. At the same time, the poorer soldiers in the Spartan army also mutinied against the aristocratic military leaders. The threat to Spartan survival was resolved by the legendary Spartan lawgiver, Lycurgus. Lycurgus promised land redistribution to the Spartan soldiers. The reunified army then crushed the rebellion of the small farmers. The defeated Messenians were reduced in status to *helots* who worked the land for the benefit of the Spartan citizens. Lycurgus also reorganized the Spartan constitution. At the head of the government were two kings advised by an aristocratic council of elders, the *gerousia*, who held office for life. The kings served as military commanders of the state army. The *gerousia* served as the state court, composed the laws, and directed the daily affairs of the *polis*. The executive branch of government was the board of *ephors*. After the constitutional reform, all Spartan male citizens were required to undergo military training from age seven to age twenty. Young trainees were paired with seasoned soldiers as advisors and lovers. At age twenty, Spartan trainees joined the *krypteia,* or secret police force, under the command of the *ephors*. Only at age thirty did Spartan men of sufficient wealth and property achieve full citizenship as *homoioi* or equals. Spartan women also underwent a course of training for childbearing. Spartan society required complete dedication to martial activities. As a result, Spartan culture was lacking in artistic and intellectual development. The Spartans also refused to participate in the commercial system connecting the Greek city-states.

D.   Democratic Athens

Until the seventh century B.C., the aristocratic clan of Alcmaeonids dominated the *polis* of Athens. The executive functions of the *polis* were carried out by a board of nine *archons* advised by an aristocratic council called the *Areopagus*. By the late seventh century B.C., Athens also experienced conflict between the aristocratic clans and the poorer citizens caused by overpopulation and deteriorating economic conditions. Around 630 B.C. an attempted tyranny failed, and a civil war ensued. In 621 B.C. the first of a series of reforms was initiated. Draco revised the Athenian codes to restore order, but failed to address the underlying political, social, and economic problems. In 594 B.C. the *archon* Solon abolished slavery for debt, although he did not radically redistribute land as had been done in Sparta. He also revised the Athenian constitution by dividing Athenians into four classes based on wealth. Service in office was opened to the two wealthiest classifications. When Solon's reforms proved insufficient to curb the oligarchy of the aristocratic families, the Athenians turned to a tyrant, Peisistratus. Peisistratus governed from 545 to his death in 527 B.C. He was briefly succeeded by his son Hippias. The tyrants redistributed land, initiated public works, and sought to strengthen the agricultural economy. They were thus popular with the small farmers of the Athenian countryside. Hippias eventually alienated a sufficient number of aristocratic clans that he was driven from power in 510 B.C. Although the aristocrats attempted to restore the oligarchy, they were not successful. Cleisthenes enacted the final reform of the Athenian constitution. As at Corinth, Cleisthenes attempted to break down the traditional clan political affiliations by dividing the Athenian city-state into three geographical units, each of which was in turn divided into ten subdivisions. Each year the citizens in the new political districts elected all public officials of the *polis*. Thus Cleisthenes' reforms established a true democracy in Athens.

V.   The Coming of Persia and the End of the Archaic Age

Greek experimentation resulted in the creation of innovative political, artistic, and intellectual forms. In the second half of the sixth century B.C., their achievements were challenged by the older civilizations of the Middle Eastern flood plains. The Persians, the successors of the Medians and New Babylonia in Mesopotamia, crushed the Greek *poleis* of the Asia Minor coast. At the outset of the fifth century B.C., the Persians prepared to extend their mastery to the Greek mainland.

TIMELINE

Insert the following events into the timeline. This should help you to compare important historical events chronologically.

beginning of Mycenaean civilization   Ionian city-states revolt
Cypselus rules in Corinth   Greek Dark Age
beginning of Minoan civilization   Solon elected archon in Athens

```
┌──  2500 B.C.
├──  1600 B.C.
├──  1200-700 B.C.
├──  650 B.C.
├──  594 B.C.
└──  499 B.C.
```

TERMS, PEOPLE, EVENTS

The following terms, people, and events are important to your understanding of the chapter. Define each one.

Iliad	Cycladic culture	Minoan culture
Mycenaean culture	Knossos	Mycenae
Dark Age	Archaic Age	*ethnos*
oligarchy	*polis*	*hoplites*
tyrant	Olympia	Delphi
myths	Ionian philosophers	*kouros*
black figure style	Cypselus	eight deliberators
equals	*helots*	*gerousia*
krypteia	*perioikoi*	Draco
Solon	Lycurgus	Peisistratus
Cleisthenes	Cyrus II	

MAP EXERCISE

The following exercise is intended to clarify the geophysical environment and the spatial relationships among the important objects and places mentioned in the chapter. Locate the following places on the map.

Cycladic culture	Minoan culture	Mycenaean culture
Olympia	Delphi	Corinth
Athens	Sparta	

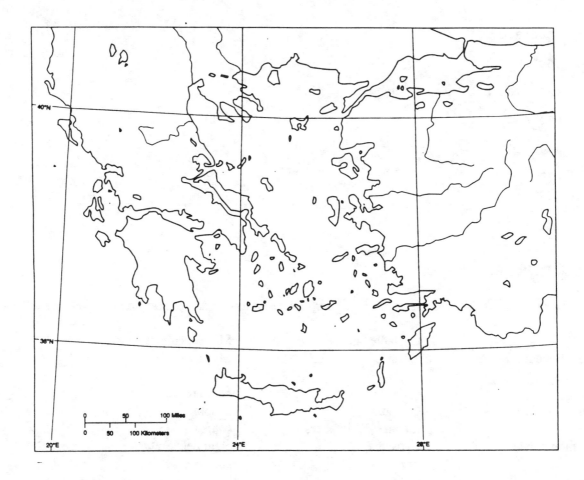

1. What prominent feature is missing from the geography of Greek civilization that was present in Egyptian, Mesopotamian, Indian, and Chinese civilizations? How did its absence affect Greek civilization?

2. What was the function of the seas in Greek civilization?

3. Where were the *poleis* concentrated? What factors may have accounted for the concentration of *poleis*?

MAKING CONNECTIONS

The following questions are intended to emphasize important ideas within the chapter.

1. How did the climate and geography of Greece contribute to the nature of Greek civilization?

2. What were the three earliest cultures in Greek civilization? Where were they located?

3. When was the Greek Dark Age? What happened to Greek culture during this period? How was society organized during this period?

4. What were the two types of political organization typical of Archaic Greece? What were the results of population growth and opposition to aristocratic power in the seventh century B.C.?

5. Describe religion and philosophy in Archaic Greece.

6. Who was responsible for the development of the Corinthian constitution? What form of constitution emerged?

7. What conditions were responsible for the development of the early Spartan constitution? What form of constitution emerged?

8. What conditions resulted in constitutional reform in Athens? Who was responsible for the development of the Athenian constitution? What form of constitution emerged?

9. What brought an end to the Archaic period in Greece?

PUTTING LARGER CONCEPTS TOGETHER

The following questions test your ability to summarize the major conclusions of the chapter.

1. What are the defining characteristics of Archaic Greek civilization? Consider political organization, religion, and philosophy. Could it be said that Greek culture was defined by a strongly centralized political system? If not, what did provide a sense of unity to Greek civilization?

2. Contrast the early civilization of Greece to those of the flood plains of the Near East (Mesopotamia and Egypt). What role did geography and climate play in determining differences? How were the forms of government different? Can you find any similarities?

SELF-TEST OF FACTUAL INFORMATION

1. The *Iliad'*s contribution to Western thought stems primarily from its

   a. emphasis on the personal struggles between Achilles and Hector.
   b. descriptions of Athenian life during the rule of Cleisthenes.
   c. concern with how people face the universal elements of human destiny.
   d. focus on the Greek belief in the virtue of one all-powerful deity.

2. Which of the following was *not* characteristic of Minoan civilization?

   a. temple/palace complexes
   b. controlled agricultural production and distribution
   c. a syllabic writing system
   d. heavily fortified cities and palaces

3. What is the most plausible explanation for the fall of Minoan civilization?

   a. volcanic eruptions on Thera or a major earthquake on Crete
   b. invasion and destruction at the hands of the mainland Greeks
   c. internal warfare coupled with socioeconomic disintegration
   d. the advent of a more dominant Near Eastern culture that gradually eroded Minoan superiority

4. Which of the following attributes was most characteristic of a *polis* ?

   a. large territorial units with small villages
   b. unfortified palace/temple complexes
   c. an *acropolis*
   d. a centralized, imperial form of government

5. All of the following challenged the traditional aristocratic rule in the late Archaic Age *except*

   a. increasing impoverishment of the rural peasants.
   b. the rise of a new class of wealthy merchants.
   c. rapid growth of the urban population.
   d. the development of a unified Greek state.

6. Which of the following statements most accurately describes the role of women in Archaic Greek society?

   a. Women shared in the public and political life of the *polis*.
   b. Women who appeared in public were mostly slaves and prostitutes.
   c. Women passed from the authority of their fathers to full membership in Greek society with marriage.
   d. Greek society condemned sexual exploitation of women and slave boys.

7. The origins of Greek philosophy can be traced to all of the following *except*

   a. contact with the Babylonian traditions of astronomy, mathematics, and science.
   b. the strong foundation of rational science left over from Achaean civilization.
   c. a group of sixth-century B.C. Ionian Greeks investigating the origins of the universe.
   d. a need to understand the universe, not through myth or religion, but by observation.

8. What Corinthian tyrant led the overthrow of the ruling Bacchiad clan around 650 B.C.?

   a. Cypselus
   b. Solon
   c. Alcibiades
   d. Peisistratus

9. Until the seventh century B.C., Athens was able to escape the civil strife prevalent in other states because

   a. its well-formed military prevented even the inkling of unrest.
   b. the democratic system already formed by the eighth century B.C. had made the people content.
   c. a policy of free immigration and universal suffrage had satisfied the diverse population.
   d. its relative abundance of land and commercial prosperity had provided stability.

10. The rise of what empire threatened the Archaic civilization of Greece?

    a. Hittite
    b. Babylonian
    c. Phoenician
    d. Persian

Chapter 3

Classical and Hellenistic Greece, 500–100 B.C.

OUTLINE

I. Alexander at Issus

The classical age of Greece began and ended with victories over the Persian Empire. The first was the unexpected triumph of the independent *poleis* over the might of Darius I. The Greek success fueled the development of Greek culture independent of the East. The second victory was even more stunning. Under the leadership of Alexander of Macedonia, Greek culture conquered the Eastern empires and beyond.

II. War and Politics in the Fifth Century B.C.

A. The Persian Wars

Darius I planned the first Persian attack on the Greek mainland as a means of punishing the Athenians for their aid to the subject city-states of Asia Minor. Without any sense of national unity, the Greek *poleis* were not united in their opposition to the Persian invader. Athens stood virtually alone against the assault in 490 B.C. Despite the odds, the Athenians under the command of Miltiades won a great victory on the plains of Marathon. In the aftermath of the victory, Athenians became convinced of the invincibility of their arms, the superiority of their culture, and the efficiency of democratic government. Further democratic reforms were instituted. Ostracism permitted the exile by popular vote of any citizen deemed likely to become too powerful. At the same time, the manner of election to almost all public office was changed to selection by lot. The second Persian invasion of the Greek mainland came nearly ten years after the first. The Emperor Xerxes mounted a combined land and sea assault on the Greek *poleis*. Although the Greek city-states were still not united, Sparta, Athens, and some others were able to construct an alliance to fend off the invasion. The Spartans sought to delay the Persian army's advance at the mountain pass at Thermopylae. King Leonidas and his three hundred equals succeeded in gaining valuable time, but paid for their success with their lives. The Persian army and navy then descended on Athens. The Athenian general Themistocles abandoned the city and moved the entire population to the island of Salamis. In the straits between the island and the mainland, Themistocles' Athenian navy won a great victory over the Persian fleet. The allied army, fighting under the command of the Spartan general Pausanias won a land engagement at Plataea. The combined successes of Athens' fleet and the Spartan army forced the Persians to withdraw in defeat.

B.   The Athenian Empire

Sparta was too preoccupied with its internal political affairs to follow up on the victory over the Persians. In contrast, the Athenians began to extend their authority over other city-states on the mainland and in the Aegean. The stated purpose for the extension of Athenian power was the continued war against the Persians. In 478 B.C. the Athenians assumed leadership of the Delian League, an alliance of *poleis* to carry on a naval war to free the Aegean and Asia Minor from Persian influence. Members of the league contributed ships or money to the treasury originally kept on the island of Delos. Over time the league, which had begun as an alliance of equals, was subverted to an Athenian empire. Monies originally intended to serve all members were transferred into the public treasury of Athens. Athens controlled the subject city-states militarily. Those who sought to withdraw from the empire were resolutely crushed, and whole populations were transported or sold into slavery.

C.   Private and Public Life in Athens

Athens was enriched by the contributions of its subject city-states. At its height its population reached about 350,000 people, only 60,000 of which were citizens. At the bottom of Athenian society were slaves, perhaps one-fourth of the total population. As in all societies, slaves were regarded as the property of their owners, but treatment of slaves varied. Generally speaking, rural slaves and those who labored in the mines were less well off. On rare occasions, slaves could and did amass private wealth. About half of the free population of Athens were people born outside the city-state of Attica. They were called *metoikoi* or metics. Many of these people came from the subject city-states of the Athenian empire, although some were non-Greek. Metics could not own land or hold public office in Athens. They were most commonly engaged in commerce, banking, and the skilled crafts in the great Athenian port of Piraeus. Women held low status in Athenian society. They were valued only for purposes of marriage, transfer of property, and procreation. They were forbidden to hold public office and generally were not part of the Athenian labor force. Although all male citizens of Athens were eligible for public office and theoretically equal, status remained a visible part of Athenian society. The majority of citizens were poor farmers. Some citizens earned their wealth through commerce, although trade and industry were largely the province of the metics. Finally, although public office had been democratized, aristocratic families continued to exert strong influence and to hold much of the real property in Attica. Equality in political life in Athens was symbolized by the *ekklesia* or assembly to which all citizens belonged. Although full meetings of the assembly did occur on rare occasions, most business was transacted in the smaller *boule* or Council of Five Hundred whose members were selected by lot from the electoral districts established in Cleisthenes' reforms. Because of the extreme democratization of office-holding in Athens, political leadership was exercised by popular leaders or demagogues. These were unelected men who practiced their control of government through their control of informal political networks, service on voluntary committees, and their personal appeal. Demagogues were often members of aristocratic families. The position of demagogue was not secure because of the Athenian practice of ostracism. Themistocles, the hero of Salamis, was ostracized as was Cimon, the son of Miltiades.

D.   Pericles and Athens

With the ostracism of the heroes of the Persian Wars, political leadership in Athens fell to Pericles. His career was typical of a demagogue: participation in popular public works projects, eloquence in public speaking, extension of democracy to all citizens regardless of property qualifications, and restriction of citizenship to native-born Athenians. Under Pericles' leadership, Athens changed the direction of its foreign policy. Athens broke its long alliance with the Spartans and began to direct the forces of its empire against the Peloponnesian rival city-state. After a lengthy period of animosity, warfare between Sparta, Athens, and their respective allies broke out in 431 B.C.

E.   The Peloponnesian War

The Peloponnesian War can be broken down into two phases: from 431 to 421 B.C. and from 414 to 404 B.C. The first phase of the conflict was a war of attrition. The Spartan army ravaged Attica outside the walls of Athens, while the Athenian fleet raided the shores of the Peloponnesus and fomented revolt amongst the Spartan *helots*. The first phase of the war was inconclusive, and the exhausted combatants agreed to a peace in 421 B.C. The Athenian leader Pericles died during an outbreak of the plague during the first stage of the war. Pericles' relative, Alcibiades, sought to succeed his kinsman as demagogue in Athens. He convinced the Athenians to extend the war to the colonies of the western Mediterranean, particularly the city-state of Syracuse on the island of Sicily. Accused of a religious offense just after his departure in the Sicilian campaign, Alcibiades abandoned his fleet. He sought refuge first with the Spartans, then with the Persians. In his absence, the Athenian campaign was a disaster and marked the beginning of the demise of the Athenian war fleet. Alcibiades sought to establish his political power base in Athens for a second time in 411 B.C. He offered to secure a Persian alliance against the Spartans in return for a change in the Athenian constitution. Briefly, an oligarchy was established, but quickly suppressed. The final Athenian defeat followed shortly thereafter. In 404 B.C. the Spartan king captured Athens and destroyed its defensive fortifications.

III.   Athenian Culture in the Hellenic Age

A.   Introduction

Much of what we consider the culture of classical Greece was actually Athenian culture. The citizens of Athens made major contributions to drama, art, and philosophy.

B.   The Examined Life

The Ionian philosophers began the exploration of the rational universe, but the Athenians raised the examination of the human to new heights. The Sophists were the first "school" of philosophy. Gorgias and Protagoras taught the skills of rhetoric and logic, mostly to young aristocrats seeking a role in public affairs. Socrates (470–399 B.C.) condemned the Sophists for their failure to examine the moral choices of public life. Socrates sought to question, literally, the moral rectitude of all public decisions and attacked the ignorance of his contemporaries. He was eventually condemned to death by the Athenian courts for corrupting the morals of youths under his instruction. Historical writing finds its origins in classical Athens. Herodotus, the chronicler of the Persian Wars, and Thucydides, the historian of the Peloponnesian War, are founders of the art of historical interpretation.

C.   Athenian Drama

Drama had long been associated in Greek culture with religious festivals. Drama was traditionally divided into the categories of tragedy, comedy, and the satyr plays. The great Athenian tragedians were Aeschylus, Sophocles, and Euripides. The authors vary in their treatment of drama. Aeschylus echoed the traditional Greek values; Sophocles emphasized the role of fate in men's lives; and Euripides dealt more directly with human emotion. The Athenian comedians dealt satirically with contemporary political events. The most famous of the Athenian comedians was Aristophanes.

D.   The Human Image

Athenian art continued to develop a more natural and less stylized form. Vase painting passed from black figure to a more lifelike and colorful rendering of human figures. Sculpture similarly sought to explore naturalism. The rebuilding of the acropolis during the time of Pericles remains the greatest expression of classical Greek sculpture.

IV.   From City-States to Macedonian Empire, 404—323 B.C.

A.   Introduction

The Peloponnesian War left a vacuum of political power on the Greek mainland. Both Sparta and Athens were exhausted. Political unification of the Greek city-states remained beyond the capability of any single *polis*.

B.   Politics After the Peloponnesian War

The Peloponnesian War altered the nature of warfare in Greece. The hoplites lost their dominance on the battlefield to lightly armed professional soldiers. The switch from hoplite to mercenary armies led to increasing numbers of war atrocities. Sparta failed to construct a lasting empire after its victory in the Peloponnesian War. Spartans established oligarchies in conquered city-states, including Athens. The clumsy attempt to alter the political configuration of Greece was rapidly overthrown, and revolts broke out everywhere against Spartan overlordship. A series of unstable alliances sought to bring down the victors of the Peloponnesian War. By 371 B.C., Thebes defeated Sparta and established its own hegemony. An alliance of *poleis* defeated Thebes, and Athens failed in its attempts to restore its former dominance. Mainland Greece remained fragmented without any political unity beyond the individual city-state in the 330s B.C.

C.   Philosophy and the Polis

The failure of Greek attempts to unify politically affected Athenian philosophers. A student of Socrates, Plato, disavowed the concept of democracy and argued for the creation of an ideal government ruled by an elite of philosophers. Plato posited the theory of Forms or Ideas, eternal and perfect concepts that exist outside the material world. Truth could only be perceived through knowledge of the forms, not their imperfect reflections in the natural world. Plato's rejection of observation in the material world was disavowed by his student, Aristotle. Aristotle constructed a system of knowledge based on close observation followed by conclusions or abstractions drawn from experiential information. According to Aristotle's examination of political structures, the best government avoided the pitfalls of both narrow oligarchy and radical democracy. Aristotle served as

25

teacher in the Macedonian court for the son of the king of Macedonia, Alexander.

D.   The Rise of Macedon

The *ethnos*, not the *polis,* was the model of government in Macedonia. The rulers of Macedonia were kings chosen from among the clan leaders. Ostensibly a Greek culture, the Macedonians existed on the frontiers of the Greek world and served as a barrier to even more primitive barbarians. Under the leadership of King Philip II, Macedonia prepared to move into the political vacuum created in the aftermath of the Peloponnesian War. Philip secured his selection to the throne by a series of assassinations. He then defeated the traditional Macedonian enemies on his borders before preparing a campaign against the Greek *poleis*. The Greek campaigns began in 346 B.C. and ended with his victory over the Greek city-states at the battle of Chaeronea in 338 B.C. To bind together his conquests, Philip created the League of Corinth. The new political unification of Greece was unlike the previous confederations of independent city-states. All league members were forced to follow the leadership of Philip as hegemon. Once Greece was finally unified under Macedonian rule, Philip prepared an invasion of the Persian Empire. Before he could initiate a campaign, he was assassinated.

E.   The Empire of Alexander the Great

Philip was succeeded by his son Alexander, who carried out his father's plans for imperial conquest. The assault on the Persian Empire began in 334 B.C. Under the brilliant generalship of the young Macedonian king, Greek armies swept through Asia Minor, Palestine, Egypt, and Persia. In three years, the Persian Empire recognized Alexander as its new leader. Alexander pressed his armies eastward from the Persian capital farther into Asia—as far as the modern states of Afghanistan and Pakistan. When his armies at last refused to continue, Alexander reluctantly returned to Persia where he died in 323 B.C. It had been Alexander's goal to merge Greek culture with the more centralized political tradition of the East, but the Macedonian empire was in many ways a personal one. After Alexander's death, strife between military commanders immediately disrupted it.

V.   The Hellenistic World

A.   Urban Life and Culture

As Alexander had proceeded on his path of conquest, he had constructed cities. Hellenistic cities were Greek in culture, architectural form, and constitution. There were, however, differences. Hellenistic cities were larger, were not independent *poleis* but subject to absolute monarchs, and were open to all residents regardless of their geographical origins. Women achieved higher status in Hellenistic society than in classical Greece. They were able to control their own property and in some areas of the Hellenistic world, particularly Egypt, were able to hold public office. The Ptolemy dynasty had a tradition of female monarchs. Hellenistic art and literature benefited from extensive patronage. Alexandria in Egypt emerged as the greatest center of scholarship in the ancient world. The romance and pastoral poem as forms of literature were creations of Hellenistic authors. With the development of larger Hellenistic cities, architectural forms became more flamboyant and monumental. Art tended toward the romantic and individual rather than the ideal.

B.   Hellenistic Philosophy

Philosophy in the Hellenistic world was dominated by three schools: the Cynics, the Epicureans, and the Stoics. The Cynics saw the material world as evil and urged followers to renounce all material possessions. The founders of the school were Antisthenes and Diogenes of Sinope. The Epicureans sought to maximize the pleasurable and to minimize pain. They taught retreat from public life and concentration on simplicity and tranquillity. The founder of the school was Epicurus. The founder of Stoicism, Zeno, believed that the entire universe was ordered according to natural laws. Each person is consigned a role in the natural system and must seek to discover and fulfill that vocation.

C.   Mathematics and Science

Hellenistic Egypt emerged as a new center of mathematics and science. Mathematics and the application of mathematics to the cosmos through astronomy were areas of special significance. The geometer Euclid created a system of geometry that continues to exist. Archimedes was renowned for his application of mathematical theory to ancient engineering. Hipparchus of Nicea created a theory of the basic order of the universe with an earth-centered cosmology that remained unchanged until the sixteenth century. Advances were also made in medicine. Although the Hellenistic rulers made many attempts to bridge the cultural gaps between the indigenous populations of their territories and the Greeks, there was often open resistance to cultural homogenization. Resistance to the imposition of Greek culture among the Jews led to rebellion after 167 B.C. Violent opposition was repeated elsewhere in the kingdoms that had once been part of Alexander's empire.

TIMELINE

Insert the following events into the timeline. This should help you to compare important historical events chronologically.

battle of Marathon
Athens assumes control of Delian League
Peloponnesian War

reign of Alexander the Great
Philip of Macedon defeats Athens
life of Aristotle

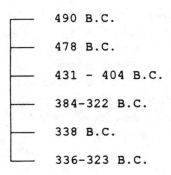

490 B.C.

478 B.C.

431 - 404 B.C.

384-322 B.C.

338 B.C.

336-323 B.C.

TERMS, PEOPLE, EVENTS

The following terms, people, and events are important to your understanding of the chapter. Define each one.

Marathon	ostracism	Thermopylae
Salamis	Persian Wars	Delian League
metics	cult of Dionysus	*ekklesia*
boule	Pericles	Thucydides
Peloponnesian War	Alcibiades	Sophists
Socrates	Herodotus	Aeschylus
Sophocles	Euripides	Aristophanes
Phidias	Athenian acropolis	Plato
Aristotle	Macedonia	Philip II
Alexander III	Ptolemy I	Seleucus
Antigonus Gonatas	Cynics	Epicureans
Stoics		

MAP EXERCISE

The following exercise is intended to clarify the geophysical environment and the spatial relationships among the important objects and places mentioned in the chapter. Locate the following places on the map.

Athens   Macedonia   the Persian Empire
the Delian League

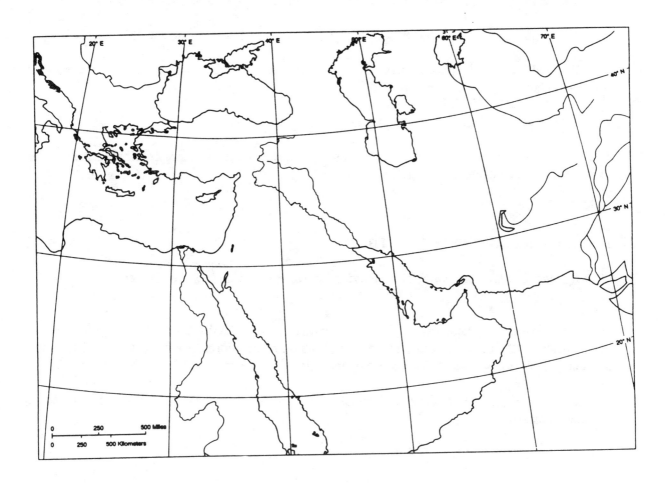

1. Until the rise of Macedonia under Philip II and Alexander III, how large were the Greek "empires"? How does the territory covered by the Delian League compare to that of the Persian Empire?

2. Considering only the area involved, is it more accurate to say that Alexander conquered the Persian Empire or that the Persian Empire finally swallowed the Greek mainland?

MAKING CONNECTIONS

The following questions are intended to emphasize important ideas within the chapter.

1. How did the victories over the Persians affect the Athenian constitution? How did they affect the relationship of Athens with other Greek *poleis*?

2. How democratic was the Athenian constitution? What groups were excluded from citizenship?

3. Discuss Athenian accomplishments in philosophy, the arts, and drama during the fifth century B.C.

4. Compare and contrast the philosophies of Plato and Aristotle. What generated such examination of Athenian culture and political organization?

5. What factors permitted the domination of Macedonia over the Greek *poleis*?

6. What did Alexander hope to accomplish with his enormous territorial conquests? How successful was he in creating a homogeneous culture in his empire?

PUTTING LARGER CONCEPTS TOGETHER

The following questions test your ability to summarize the major conclusions of the chapter.

1. One of the clearest differences between Greek civilization and other civilizations we have considered and will consider is the failure to establish any long-lasting imperial form of government. What factors account for Greek civilization's inability to maintain imperial government?

2. What is the final significance of Greek civilization? How did Greek civilization have a lasting impact on subsequent history?

SELF-TEST OF FACTUAL INFORMATION

1. Which of the following was *not* true of the Athenian victory over the Persians in 490 B.C.?

    a. It established the superiority of the hoplite phalanx.
    b. It convinced Greeks of their cultural superiority over barbarians.
    c. It enhanced the democratic reforms of Cleisthenes.
    d. It ended all Persian hopes of successfully invading Greece.

2. Which of the following statements concerning the Delian League is most accurate?

    a. It was disbanded after the Athenian victory over the Persians in Egypt in 454 B.C.
    b. It was converted into an Athenian empire.
    c. It consisted of Sparta and Athens as well as a few of the Athenian colonies.
    d. It was initially intended by Athens as a potential alliance against the Spartans.

3. Most of the leaders of fifth-century Athens came from the

    a. ranks of the metics.
    b. aristocracy, the ranks of old wealth and influence.
    c. rural population of farmers.
    d. ranks of the ostracized.

4. The Peloponnesian War

    a. marked the continuation of the Athenian and Spartan alliance against the Persians.
    b. resulted in the Spartan defeat of Athens and the imposition of an oligarchy on the defeated city.
    c. resulted in the Athenian defeat of Sparta and the inclusion of Sparta in the Athenian empire.
    d. resulted in the defeat of both Sparta and Athens by Corinth.

5. Which of the following statements does *not* accurately describe Herodotus' history of the Persian Wars?

    a. He believed that the gods intervened directly in human affairs.
    b. He repeated myths, legends, and outrageous tales.
    c. He described the Persian Wars as a conflict between freedom and despotism.
    d. He failed to demonstrate even a rudimentary understanding of cause and effect in history.

6. Which of the following was a major Greek dramatist?

    a. Aeschylus
    b. Thucydides
    c. Pericles
    d. Socrates

7. Which of the following statements best describes Plato's political views?

   a. He demanded increased democratization of the constitution.
   b. He was satisfied with the government as it existed in Athens during his lifetime.
   c. He advocated creation of a government ruled by a philosopher elite.
   d. He suggested a balance between oligarchy and democracy.

8. Which of the following statements concerning Philip II of Macedonia is *not* accurate?

   a. Philip established the League of Corinth, effectively a Macedonian empire in the Greek mainland.
   b. Philip's success was based on his prowess as a military commander.
   c. Philip was content with the conquest of the Greek mainland and intended no further campaigns.
   d. Philip was assassinated at age forty-six, leaving his son Alexander as his successor.

9. Which of the following schools of philosophy was *not* prevalent in the Hellenistic period?

   a. Cynicism
   b. Stoicism
   c. Existentialism
   d. Epicureanism

10. In what way was Alexander's creation of a Hellenistic world limited?

    a. Alexander never was able to establish cities in any way similar to those of the Greek mainland.
    b. Hellenistic science and mathematics failed to blend Greek and Near Eastern ideas.
    c. Hellenistic art forms were never adopted outside of Greece and Macedonia.
    d. Indigenous populations often rejected the imposition of Greek culture to the extent of rebellion.

Chapter 4

Early Rome and the Roman Republic, 800–31 B.C.

OUTLINE

I.   Eternal Rome

Rome was literally built on a series of elevated hills on the banks of the Tiber River. The original agricultural villages on each hill eventually coalesced into a single settlement. Each hill served a separate function. The Palatine was the preferred residential district. The Capitoline, the acropolis of Rome, was the religious center. Between the hills was the public meeting place or Forum. Here the political, religious, and commercial structures marked the advance of Roman civilization.

II.   The Western Mediterranean to 509 B.C.

A.   Introduction

Civilization began later in the western Mediterranean than in the flood plains of the East. A Bronze Age culture did not develop until 1500 B.C. Rich in metallic ores, the western Mediterranean developed as a source of ores and metallurgy. Around 1000 B.C., the Villanovan civilization, an iron-using culture, replaced the earlier Bronze Age cultures in northern Italy. At about the same time, other peoples speaking a different tongue, Italic, migrated into Italy.

B.   The Merchants of Baal

Around 800 B.C., the Phoenicians established a series of trading bases tying together the Phoenician home cities of Tyre, Byblos, and Sidon on the eastern coast of the Mediterranean with commercial centers located in northern Africa, Italy, Spain, and the Mediterranean islands. The greatest of the Phoenician commercial centers in the western Mediterranean was Carthage in northern Africa. Carthage became independent of the Phoenician homeland when the mother cities fell to the New Babylonian Empire in the sixth century B.C. Carthage built a commercial empire in the western Mediterranean. Fertile agricultural hinterlands supported the growth of the city, and armies recruited from various ethnic groups throughout the western Mediterranean protected the far-flung ports of trade. The constitution of Carthage was mixed. A popular assembly annually elected heads of state, but the candidates were limited to the commercial aristocracy. The heads of state were advised by an equally aristocratic senate. Military commanders were also elected. The government was, thus, not democratic and there was little popular involvement. Carthaginian religion was derived from the Phoenicians. The chief god was Baal. Carthaginians may have been forced to sacrifice their first-born male children to Baal.

C.   The Western Greeks

Greek colonization of the western Mediterranean began in the eighth century B.C. Greek colonies were concentrated in the island of Sicily and on the southern mainland of Italy, called Greater Greece. Syracuse was one of the greatest colonial ventures. Initially Greek colonization posed no threat to Carthaginian territories; but as the Greek migration continued, the two cultures came into conflict. In the fifth century B.C., the rulers of Syracuse were successful in defeating Carthaginian assaults. The success of the Greek colonists in defending their settlements permitted a half-century of cultural advance. In 410 B.C. the wars between Carthage and the Sicilian colonies resumed with inconclusive results.

D.   Italy's First Civilization

The first Italian civilization was that of the Etruscans. The Etruscans were probably descendants of the Villanovan culture. The script of the Etruscans was derived from the Greek alphabet, although the languages are entirely different. In the mid-sixth century B.C., twelve tribal groups sharing a similar language and culture united to form a confederation to oppose the continued advance of Greek colonization. Eventually the Etruscan confederation came to include many settlements in the Italian peninsula. Cities, each ruled by a king, were the political units of the confederacy. By the fifth century B.C., the kingship evolved into oligarchic governments dominated by aristocratic assemblies. The assemblies elected magistrates responsible for the administration of the cities. This was the basis for the later Roman republican form of government. Etruscan society was typified by two status groups: a land-owning aristocracy and slave laborers. Women held relatively high status in Etruscan society and were active in public life. The Etruscans, like the Greek colonies and the Carthaginians, sought to establish a commercial hegemony. At the end of the sixth century B.C., the Etruscan cities, including Rome, entered into an alliance with the Carthaginians directed against their common Greek enemies. The Etruscans fared poorly in the war against the Greek colonies. Their defeat marked the beginning of Etruscan decline which continued throughout the fifth century B.C.

III.   From City of Rome to the Roman Empire, 509—146 B.C.

A.   Introduction

Early Romans saw themselves as simple farmers and citizen-soldiers. They constructed myths of ideal political role models: Cincinnatus, Horatius Cocles, and Lucretia. They also constructed origin myths to explain the beginnings of Roman society. The stories of Romulus and Remus, the Homeric tradition of Aeneas, and the mythic histories of Etruscan kings established the foundations of Roman destiny.

B.   Latin Rome

Latium, the homeland of the Latins, lay between Etruria to the north and Greater Greece to the south. By the end of the seventh century B.C., a cluster of villages on the hills near the Tiber River formed a league for military defense and shared religious cults. This group of villages became Rome. At the foundation of early Roman society were households dominated by a *paterfamilias* with power of life and death over household members. Related households were grouped into clans or *gentes*. Those households unrelated to *gentes* were referred to as *plebeian*, while the members of clans were called *patricians*. Heads of the patrician families composed an aristocratic council, the Senate. In addition to the Senate, an assembly of all male citizens selected kings. Kingship was largely a ritual position.

C.   Etruscan Rome

In the middle of the seventh century B.C., the Etruscans overwhelmed the Romans and added them to the Etruscan confederacy. Etruscan kings and magistrates, more powerful than their Roman counterparts, were introduced into the Roman political structure. Rome became an important part of the Etruscan trade network and expanded as its economic significance grew. The Etruscans also reorganized Roman social structure. As in Greece, the democratization of the military through the introduction of hoplite infantry created a social system based on land-holding. The Etruscan King Servius Tullius divided Roman society into five groups according to landed wealth and their ability to serve militarily. Each group was divided into centuries. Members of the centuries composed a new political assembly, the centuriate assembly, which took over the task of electing the magistrates. The wealthy landowning aristocracy dominated the centuriate assembly. Gradually the patricians assumed a monopoly over public office. The Etruscans significantly altered the politics, society, and economy of Rome; but they were unable to maintain their dominance. Around 509 B.C., the Romans expelled the Etruscan kings and established a new government.

D.   Rome and Italy

The expulsion of the Etruscan kings is part of the Roman myth of origin. The establishment of oligarchy was typical of all Italian political structures. The early republic was a patrician monopoly of power. At the top of the government were two consuls elected in the centuriate assembly for one-year terms. Over time, other magistrates were developed to aid the consuls in the administration of the government. Praetors, quaestors, and censors formed a college of magistrates. The ladder of political office was called the *cursus honorum*. The Senate was transformed into a body of former magistrates who advised the consuls. The centuriate assembly proposed laws and elected magistrates to annual office. Patrician families also controlled the major public priesthoods. Excluded from the government, the plebeian families withdrew from the Roman republic and military service in the first half of the fifth century. The plebeians formed their own representative and legislative assembly, the Council of the Plebs. The plebeian magistrates, charged with protecting the interests of the plebs, were called tribunes. By the middle of the fifth century B.C., there were parallel patrician and plebeian political structures. An assault from a nearby town caused the patricians to seek a compromise with the plebeians. In 450 B.C. a written law code, the Twelve Tables, guaranteed the rights of all freemen, patrician and plebeian. The Council of the Plebs was absorbed into the Roman republic along with the office of tribune. Plebeians were eventually admitted to all of the magistracies and the priesthoods. With the settlement of the Struggle of Orders, the Roman republic was free to embark of a program of military conquest in Italy. Between 396 B.C. and 265 B.C., Roman legions successfully defeated all of their Italian neighbors, including the Etruscans and the colonies of Greece. Some conquered territory was turned over to Roman colonists. Conquered populations were either admitted to Roman citizenship or offered the status of allies. These policies bound the formerly alien populations to the fortunes of Rome and drew them into the Roman political and cultural system.

E.   Rome and the Mediterranean

As a member of the Etruscan confederacy, Rome was initially an ally of the Carthaginians. Even with the development of the Roman republic, the Romans posed no threat to Carthage because of their lack of a navy. The conquest of the Greek colonies on the Italian mainland, however, attracted Roman interest in Sicily. With the attempted conquest of Sicily, Rome came into conflict with traditional Carthaginian imperial interests. Rome and Carthage fought three Punic Wars, all of them Roman victories. The First Punic War (265–241 B.C.) resulted in the Roman conquest of Sicily and in the development of a Roman war fleet. The Second Punic War (218–202 B.C.) broke out over disputed colonization of Spain, claimed by both Rome and Carthage. The great Carthaginian general, Hannibal, successfully crossed the Italian Alps and invaded Italy. Despite a series of brilliant military victories over a period of fourteen years, Hannibal could not break the Roman system of Italian alliances. Under the command of the consul Publius Cornelius Scipio, Rome struck first at Spain and then at Carthage itself. The Roman assault on northern Africa forced Hannibal's withdrawal from Italy. He was finally defeated at Zama in 202 B.C. Carthage was forced to cede its entire empire to Rome as a result of the defeat. In the Third Punic War (149–146 B.C.), the Romans guaranteed that Carthage could never again threaten Roman intentions in the western Mediterranean. The city of Carthage was destroyed. At about the same time as the end of the Punic Wars, the Romans had extended their political interests into the eastern half of the Mediterranean. In a series of wars, the Romans were able to intervene in the internecine squabbles of the Hellenistic successor states of Alexander's empire. The Romans defeated the Antigonids of Macedonia and the Seleucids of Asia Minor. By 146 B.C., the Romans controlled Greece and the coast of Asia Minor. The Roman republican empire covered the entire coast of the western Mediterranean, Greece, and Asia Minor.

IV. Republican Civilization

A. Introduction

The conquest of empire destroyed the social foundations of the Roman republic. The independent farmer began to disappear under the new economic conditions.

B. Farmers and Soldiers

The backbone of the Roman military and the source of its citizens was the class of small, independent landowners. The Roman military, like that of classical Greece, was predominantly infantry. The Romans, however, replaced the phalanx with the more maneuverable legion. In addition to a more maneuverable formation, the Romans also supplemented their military with feats of engineering: bridge building, siege machines, and catapults. The creation of the republican empire destroyed the farmers on which the Roman army depended. Service at increasingly great distances from Rome made family farms unworkable. Gradually the Roman aristocracy began to assert a monopoly over real property. The small farmers sank into poverty.

C. The Roman Family

A male patriarch, the *paterfamilias*, governed the Roman household including family members, servants, and slaves. The authority of the household head was absolute, even over married male children. The creation of the republican empire caused changes in the Roman household. Women appear to have achieved greater independence. The gulf between poor and rich households increased. Multi-family dwellings became more common for the landless poor who began to flock to the cities.

D. Roman Religion

The Romans worshipped a large number of deities. Each household venerated its *lares* and *penates*, protective gods of the home and field. Beyond the household, colleges of priests undertook the responsibility of public worship. The priesthoods held no special status and were normally composed of Roman citizens. The extension of the Roman republican empire caused new deities to enter the public realm of worship. Unlike traditional Roman religions, some of the imported cults—the Greek cult of Dionysus, for example—utilized secret rites and identified ritual priesthoods. The Roman Senate occasionally suppressed these foreign religions.

E.   Republican Letters

Prior to the third century B.C., the Romans lacked an indigenous literature. In the absence of native authors, Greek historians wrote the first annals of Rome. Greek models inspired the first Roman attempts at drama. Terence and Plautus wrote Roman comedies on the Greek model.

V.   The Price of Empire, 146-121 B.C.

The conquest of new territories destroyed the Roman republic. Traditional Roman culture, society, economy, and government all gave way to a new, imperial Rome. Magistrates and commanders operating far from Rome took opportunities to enrich themselves. Ordinary citizens became increasingly cynical about the government and fearful of the power of the wealthy. Tensions between the classes led to civil war. Cato the Elder, often portrayed as the representative of traditional order in the Roman republic, attacked aspects of Roman culture imitative of Greek civilization and anything that departed from Roman frugality. Despite his public call for a return to tradition, Cato's own writing demonstrated his debt to Hellenistic culture. Like other Roman patricians, he acted to gain a share of the wealth generated by the empire.

TIMELINE

Insert the following events into the timeline. This should help you to compare important historical events chronologically.

battle of Zama	reign of Servius Tullius, Etruscan military reformer
Third Punic War	Law of Twelve Tables
First Punic War begins	expulsion of last Etruscan king

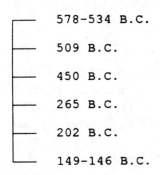

578-534 B.C.

509 B.C.

450 B.C.

265 B.C.

202 B.C.

149-146 B.C.

TERMS, PEOPLE, EVENTS

The following terms, people, and events are important to your understanding of the chapter. Define each one.

Forum	Villanovan culture	Phoenicians
Carthage	Etruscan civilization	*gentes*
curiae	*paterfamilias*	plebeians
patricians	clientage	Senate
King Servius Tullius	consuls	dictator
tribunes	Law of the Twelve Tables	Punic Wars
Hannibal	Pyrrhus of Epirus	Publius Cornelius Scipio
Cato the Elder	Roman legions	*lares familiares*
penates	Polybius	Plautus and Terence

MAP EXERCISE

The following exercise is intended to clarify the geophysical environment and the spatial relationships among the important objects and places mentioned in the chapter. Locate the following places on the map.

Rome   Carthage   boundaries of Roman republican empire
Macedonia   Pergamum

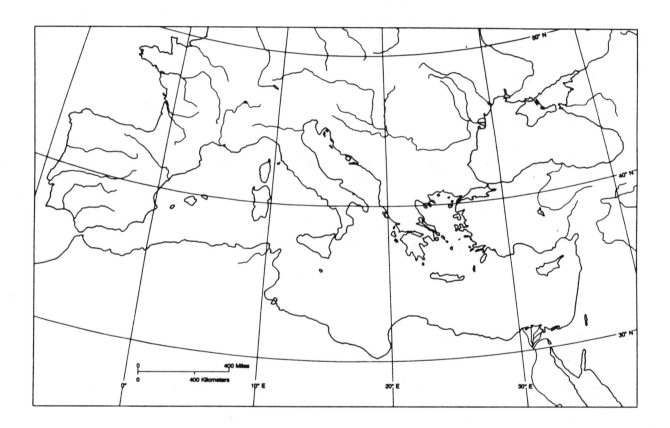

1. The text divides Roman imperial conquests into western and eastern. What does the configuration of the Mediterranean suggest about the division of Roman conquests? Why was Carthage the first natural rival for colonial dominance?

2. How does the extent of the Roman republican empire compare to the size of the Delian League of Athens? How does it compare to Alexander the Great's empire? [See Chapter 3]

MAKING CONNECTIONS

The following questions are intended to emphasize important ideas within the chapter.

1. Compare and contrast the territories and governments of the three earliest powers in the western Mediterranean—Carthage, the Greek colonies, and the Etruscans.

2. What was the social and political organization of Latin Rome? How did the Etruscans transform early Rome?

3. What was the political constitution of the early Roman republic? How did Rome's treatment of its external enemies lead to imperialism?

4. Discuss the significance of the Punic Wars. How did their outcomes affect Rome's position as an imperial power?

5. What was the structure of the Roman family and religion during the republic?

6. What stresses did the accumulation of imperial territories place on Roman social and political organization?

PUTTING LARGER CONCEPTS TOGETHER

The following questions test your ability to summarize the major conclusions of the chapter.

1. What characteristics made the creation of the republican empire possible? What characteristics made it fail?

2. One of the primary differences between Greek civilization and Roman civilization was the enormous difficulty the Greeks experienced in creating a centralized form of government that included all of Greece. The Romans, in contrast, created an imperial form of government almost immediately after their departure from Etruscan tutelage. What factors account for the differences between these two civilizations?

SELF-TEST OF FACTUAL INFORMATION

1. In what way did the Etruscans differ most significantly from the Greeks and later Romans?

   a. their establishment of a political confederation
   b. the elevated status of Etruscan women
   c. development of city organization over tribal structures
   d. incorporation of religious and legal functions of kings into civic administration

2. The original meaning of plebeian was

   a. families not organized into *gentes*.
   b. families engaged in trade rather than warfare.
   c. families that were forbidden to participate in the *curiae*.
   d. single males who were not household heads.

3. Governmental institutions of the early Roman republic developed within a context of

   a. patrician supremacy.
   b. plebeian supremacy.
   c. multi-ethnic governance shared by Greeks, Latins, and Etruscans.
   d. Theban domination.

4. What officers replaced the kings in the republican constitution of Rome?

   a. censors
   b. quaestors
   c. tribunes
   d. consuls

5. Rome was saved during the Second Punic War by all of the following *except* which factor?

   a. Most of Rome's allies continued to support the republic.
   b. The unity of all Roman classes and factions during the period remained firm.
   c. Scipio Africanus' brilliant diversionary tactics were instrumental in saving Rome.
   d. The Carthaginians were unable to mount an attack on Italy.

6. Why did the Roman republic launch military operations in the eastern Mediterranean in the second century B.C.?

   a. They were concerned about Carthaginian colonies there.
   b. They were drawn into conflicts among the successor states of Alexander the Great's empire.
   c. They wished to conquer Egypt.
   d. They responded to a Phoenician invasion of Sicily.

7. The nature of imperial expansion made the typical Roman citizen-soldier

    a. a beneficiary of the newly acquired Mediterranean lands.
    b. extraordinarily wealthy.
    c. an economic loser who was occasionally forced to give up eligibility for public service.
    d. an object of terrorist attack by various patrician forces.

8. Roman religion as defined by the state

    a. was monotheistic.
    b. excluded all foreign gods.
    c. supported a special caste of priests.
    d. sought to persecute the cult of Dionysus.

9. Roman conquest of the Mediterranean world

    a. guaranteed the success of the republican institutions.
    b. resulted in universal citizenship for all residents.
    c. spelled the end of the republican system.
    d. resulted in widespread benefits shared equally by all Romans.

10. Who was the greatest of the Greek historians to record Rome's rise to power?

    a. Plautus
    b. Terence
    c. Herodotus
    d. Polybius

Chapter 5

Imperial Rome, 27 B.C.–A.D. 192

OUTLINE

I.   Competitive Consumption

The creation of the empire marked the extension of Roman culture throughout the Mediterranean. One aspect of that culture, in addition to the traditional values defined by martial vigor, was an increasing emphasis on opulence and conspicuous consumption. The empire seemed less socially restrictive in offering its pleasures to those willing to support its expansion. The problem that the empire had to face in the long run was how to maintain its traditional values in a world more attuned to opulence and pleasure.

II.   The Price of Empire

A.   Introduction

The republican empire destroyed the way of life on which the Roman republic had been based. Hellenistic culture proved an irresistible lure. The Roman government proved powerless to prevent its oligarchs from pressing home their economic advantages to the detriment of the poorer citizens. The result was a century of revolutionary change.

B.   Winners and Losers

The real winners in the Roman defeat of Carthage and Macedonia were the members of the aristocratic oligarchy or *optimates*. They continued to exercise a monopoly of political and economic power. The conquests enriched others as well. Merchants, slave traders, and bankers flooded into the newly added territories. Those able to amass wealth in the new empire became *equites* or knights. The newly wealthy entrepreneurs served the government as tax collectors, positions used to amass even greater amounts of money. The most fortunate of the *equites* were able to enter the lower magistracies and even the Senate. Four groups suffered as a result of the imperial conquests: 1) those taken as slaves, 2) the conquered provincials, 3) the noncitizen Italian allies, and 4) the small landholders and free craftsmen who had once been the backbone of Roman society. The number of slaves in Roman society increased dramatically after the imperial conquests. Slaves replaced free labor on huge agricultural estates. The conditions under which slaves were held deteriorated rapidly, setting off a series of slave revolts between 135 B.C. and 71 B.C. All slave rebellions were doomed to failure. Rebellion was also common among the defeated provincials. In Pergamum and Pontus, both states in Asia Minor, serious revolts against Roman authority broke out. Closer to home, the Italian allies resented the failure of the Senate to extend full citizenship to all residents of Italy. Frustration led to two revolts. The most serious was the Italian Social War from 91 B.C. to 89 B.C.

C.   *Optimates* and *Populares*

The most desperate decline in status occurred among Roman citizens, the small landowners. Many lost their farms to wealthy aristocrats. Others saw the value of their work diminished by the flood of slave labor. The widespread demise of the independent family farm led to an exodus to the cities, particularly Rome. A tribune, Tiberius Gracchus, sought to relieve the problem by taking previously public land from the rich and redistributing it to the poor. Gracchus sought to have his proposal ratified in the plebeian assembly, where the tribune ran roughshod over all opposition. Gracchus also proposed other reforms in favor of the rural poor. Politicians who favored breaking the political and economic grip of the wealthy *optimates* were called *populares*. Fearing that the tribune's appeal to the masses was intended to break the power of the oligarchy, a group of senators assassinated Tiberius Gracchus. The attempt to pass reform in favor of the poor was renewed by Tiberius' brother, Gaius. Gaius Gracchus renewed the program of land redistribution, proposed granting citizenship to all Italians, and tried to bring the *equites* into the constitution as a counterbalance to the senators. Like his brother before him, Gaius Gracchus was seen as a threat to the monopoly of the senators. At the end of his term of office, the Senate removed Gaius Gracchus as a threat through assassination.

III.   The End of the Republic

A.   Introduction

Although the murders of the Gracchi seemed to put an end to political unrest, the Romans had failed to resolve the constitutional crisis.

B.   The Crisis of Government

Under the consul and military commander Marius, the tendency to private armies became problematic. Marius first rose to favor as a victor in wars in North Africa and northern Italy. He raised armies for his wars by recruiting from the mass of rural poor and disregarding the traditional property requirements for military service. As Marius promised rewards of land for service, his troops transferred their loyalty from the state to the commander. Personal armies became political tools in the late republic. The Italian Social War gave opportunities for both Marius and Sulla to raise personal armies. The two commanders became political rivals—Marius as a member of the *populares*, Sulla as a member of the *optimates*. Their rivalry became open conflict, and each commander led military assaults on the city of Rome. Both engaged in mass executions of political opponents. Sulla emerged victorious after Marius' death. With the support of the senatorial elite, Sulla was elected dictator for three years, 82 B.C. to 79 B.C. Sulla expanded the Senate, reduced the authority of the plebeian tribunes, excluded *equites* from the juries of Roman courts, and weakened the military power of magistrates. Having carried out his reforms, Sulla resigned as dictator. His reforms restored oligarchic rule, but failed to resolve the critical gulf between rich and poor.

C.   The Civil Wars

Marcus Tullius Cicero represented one type of Roman politician. Although newly admitted to the ruling class, Cicero identified entirely with the *optimates*. Although Cicero served as consul, he was strictly a politician and had no military experience. Military commanders such as Pompey, Crassus, and Julius Caesar represented greater threats to the constitution. All were protégés of Sulla, but achieved political support as *populares*. Pompey's success as a military commander ensured his political rise. Crassus was more dependent on personal wealth than military success. Caesar began his career as a follower of Crassus. Eventually all three began to cooperate in a political alliance, the First Triumvirate. As his reward, Caesar received a military command in Gaul where he achieved a series of brilliant victories. Crassus' death in 53 B.C. left only Pompey and Caesar. The two became bitter rivals. The contest for political superiority erupted in civil war in 49 B.C. Within one year, Caesar successfully defeated Pompey and removed him as a political rival. As the military survivor, Caesar was recognized as the political leader of Rome. He embarked on a series of reforms: adding Italians to the Senate and increasing its overall number to nine hundred, founding colonies for retired soldiers and those in need of land, and increasing the number of magistracies to broaden political participation. Caesar had himself declared perpetual dictator. Because Caesar clearly did not intend to restore the oligarchic republic, a group of senators assassinated him in 44 B.C. Caesar's death set off another round of civil wars. The Second Triumvirate—Antony, Lepidus, and Caesar's grandnephew and adopted son, Octavian—sought to eliminate the senators responsible for the murder of the dictator. They succeeded in 43 B.C. The three then divided command of the Roman Empire, but shared authority was only a temporary expedient. While Lepidus was permitted to retire, Antony and Octavian fought for supreme command. The contest resulted in the total victory of Octavian and the death of Antony and his supporter, Cleopatra, Queen of Egypt.

D. The Good Life

Although the last years of the republic were violent, Roman culture flourished. Cicero embodied the Roman acceptance of Stoicism. His belief in divine providence, morality, and duty was reflected in the idealism of his political career. The same concern for justice and morality can be discovered in the works of two important Roman historians, Sallust and Livy. Sallust's popular political viewpoint condemned the senators for their failings, while the more conservative Livy blamed the civil disorder on all those who departed from Roman republican traditions. The poetry of Lucretius also reflected the influence of Hellenistic philosophy. Lucretius presented Epicurean materialism as the proper goal for society. He counseled avoidance of the irrational and emotional. A different poetic style appeared in the "new-style poets," best represented by Catullus. He avoided questions of morality or political rectitude and tried to express the emotional reality of love. Realism and a concern with the individual suffused the art of republican Rome. Sculpture and art utilized the ideal body conventions of Hellenistic art, but portrayed the heads of the subjects as individual portraits.

IV. The Augustan Age

A. Introduction

Octavian established the Roman Empire, but he did so gradually and without seeming to overthrow the republican traditions. In 27 B.C., Octavian restored the republican offices and received the title Augustus. He maintained power after 27 B.C. by holding first the office of consul, then tribune. He was also granted command over the frontier provinces of the empire. This subtle absolutism worked well for Augustus and his successors.

B. The Empire Renewed

Key to the establishment of the empire was the Senate. Its membership became hereditary, and admission to its ranks was opened to more men, including Italians. The reformed Senate achieved more powers, but remained subservient to the dictates of the emperor. Augustus also rebuilt the ranks of the equites. The men of this rank filled the officer corps of the legions and served in the imperial administration. In contrast, the equites no longer served as the body of tax collectors. Critical to the restoration of order was the pacification of unrest within the army. Thirty-two legions received lands in colonies far from Rome. The practice of granting lands and pensions to soldiers after their term of service (20 years) became customary. To control the city of Rome, Augustus enrolled an elite military force, the praetorian guard, responsible for the protection of the emperor. While the reforms were effective, the problem of poverty continued to grow, especially within the cities. The emperors chose to gloss over the social crisis by providing free food and entertainment for the masses.

C.   Divine Augustus

Augustus attempted to restore the traditional values of Roman society. As a means of cultivating piety, the emperor reinvigorated the ancient cults and priesthoods. His only innovation in this area was the establishment of the cult of the emperors. Augustus also desired to bring back the typical Roman family unit, including the exclusive powers of the paterfamilias. The emperor encouraged fidelity and chastity, even when his own family provided poor examples. The emperor personally patronized those authors who shared his conservative views. Two of his favorite authors were the poets Virgil and Horace. Horace virtually venerated Augustus. Virgil's most famous work, the *Aeneid*, created a new origin myth for Roman civilization based on Homeric legend. Those writers who did not share the emperor's political and philosophical views were subject to censorship and suppression. Ovid, the Roman master of eroticism, was exiled.

D.   Augustus's Successors

Augustus was never able to provide for an orderly system of succession to the powers of the emperor. He was succeeded by a number of relatives, the Julio-Claudians, none of whom were particularly popular. The continued smooth operation of the empire despite incompetence and disorder at the top of the government testified to the success of Augustus' constitutional changes. The last member of the Julio-Claudians, Nero, committed suicide in the face of a general revolution of the armies. After a period of civil war to determine a successor, the members of the Flavian dynasty ruled from 69 to 96 A.D. The Flavians were efficient, if unspectacular. During this dynasty, the last artificial trappings of the republic were removed.

V.   The Pax Romana

A.   Introduction

The Antonine emperors followed the Flavians. These emperors (not truly a dynasty, as the emperors were adopted by their predecessors) extended the borders of the empire to their greatest limits.

B.   Administering the Empire

The government of the empire was essentially oppressive. It demanded a full range of wealth, goods, and services from its subjects. In many provinces, the native elite continued to exercise authority in the name of the emperor in return for the gift of Roman citizenship. In the imperial provinces under the direct command of the emperor, the legions provided much of the force behind the administration. The last elements of imperial administration were the households of the Roman elite, including the household of the emperor. Minions of the emperor's household, regardless of status of birth, commanded those vast territories belonging personally to the ruler.

C.   The Origins of Christianity

While participation in the traditional Roman cults was considered an act of patriotism, many residents of the empire embraced newer forms of religion. Judaism, which demanded absolute obedience to the principle of exclusive monotheism, could not be incorporated into the polytheism typical of Roman religious practice. At first, the Romans were tolerant of the special demands of Jewish religion and exempted the Jews from the public cults. Jews, themselves, were divided into those willing to admit newer Roman religious traditions (Sadducees) and those who insisted on strict separation (Hasidim and Pharisees). One member of the latter group, Hillel, began the process of legal and scriptural interpretation that became the Talmud. The most radical of the separationists, the Zealots, plotted revolt to free the Jews from Roman influence. Jewish relationships with Rome were complicated by Christ's messianic claims. The Roman procurator determined that Christ represented a political disturbance and had him executed. Christ's followers claimed that he rose from the dead and initiated a new religion, Christianity. During the missionary expeditions of Paul of Tarsus, the new religion spread beyond the Judaic communities to Asia Minor, Greece, and Rome. Christians shared with Jews the dedication to monotheism and refused to participate in the public cults of Roman religion, including the worship of the deified emperor. Under Nero, persecution of Christians began. Persecutions failed to halt the growth of the new religion within the empire. As the religion grew in numbers and as it became clear that the anticipated end of the world was not near at hand, Christians sought a more formal organization. In each community, bishops emerged as leaders responsible for both order and administration of the early sacraments. As Jesus did not, himself, leave a written text, authority within the new Church was based on Gospels, early letters, and visionary writings of the early disciples and their followers. Bishops connected these with Jewish texts to provide a basis for belief and Christian instruction. Bishops also took up responsibility for defending Christianity from external attacks and for settling internal disputes over interpretations of belief and scripture. Bishops of the most ancient Christian communities—Rome, Constantinople, Antioch, Alexandria, and Jerusalem—emerged as the most powerful officials of the Church. The elevation of the bishop within the Christian community corresponded to the separation of the priesthood from the laity and to the exclusion of women from positions of authority.

D.   A Tour of the Empire

Cities remained the bastions of Roman culture within the empire. They were connected by one of the wonders of Roman engineering, the Roman roads, the arteries of Roman administration. From A.D. 120 to A.D. 131, the emperor Hadrian traveled the Roman roads and visited every corner of his far-flung empire. Despite his odyssey, weaknesses began to appear in the imperial structure: 1) the extensive frontiers were often under attack, 2) the professional legions were becoming progressively less Roman and more provincial, 3) corruption was rampant in the administration, and 4) city and countryside remained culturally separated.

E.   The Culture of Antonine Rome

History and philosophy were important aspects of the literature of imperial Rome. Cornelius Tacitus described the intrigues of the imperial court and contrasted the Roman machinations with the simpler life of Germanic and British society. Suetonius and Plutarch wrote a series of biographies that highlighted both traditional values and more scandalous activities. Stoicism was the philosophical school that enjoyed popularity in the second century A.D. Epictetus was the most influential Stoic philosopher. The allure of Stoicism even penetrated the imperial palace, for the emperor Marcus Aurelius adopted the philosophy.

TIMELINE

Insert the following events into the timeline. This should help you to compare important historical events chronologically.

assassination of Julius Caesar   Tiberius Gracchus introduced land reform
death of Jesus   reign of Augustus
beginning of Social War   election of Gaius Marius as consul

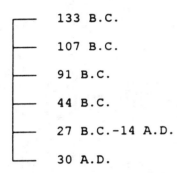

133 B.C.

107 B.C.

91 B.C.

44 B.C.

27 B.C.-14 A.D.

30 A.D.

TERMS, PEOPLE, EVENTS

The following terms, people, and events are important to your understanding of the chapter. Define each one.

optimates	*equites*	Spartacus
Social War	Tiberius Gracchus	Gaius Gracchus
populares	Gaius Marius	Marcus Tullius Cicero
Sulla	Pompey	Crassus
Julius Caesar	First Triumvirate	Antony
Octavian	Second Triumvirate	Sallust
Livy	Lucretius	Catullus
Augustus	*princeps*	*pax Romana*
Horace	Virgil	Ovid
Julio-Claudian dynasty	Flavian dynasty	Sadducees
Pharisees	Hasidim	Hillel
Zealots	Jesus of Nazareth	Peter
Paul of Tarsus	Cornelius Tacitus	Epictetus

MAP EXERCISE

The following exercise is intended to clarify the geophysical environment and the spatial relationships among the important objects and places mentioned in the chapter. Locate the following places on the map.

the Rhine-Danube frontier of the Empire   Hadrian's Wall

the Sahara frontier   the eastern frontier

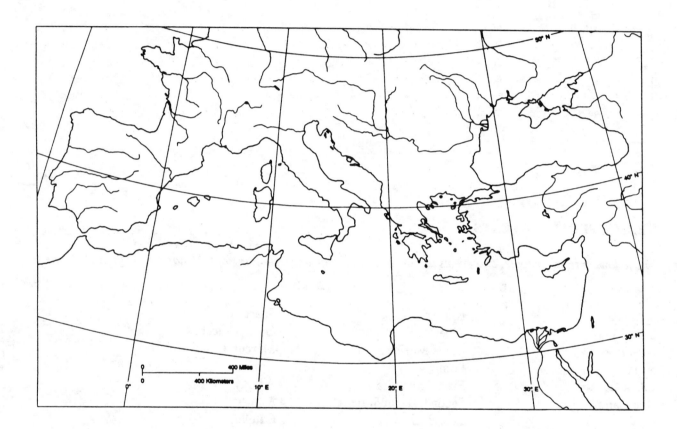

1.   Which of the frontiers of the Roman Empire was the longest? Which of the frontiers was potentially the most dangerous? Why?

2.   How did the issue of the frontier affect the Roman Empire? Consider Hadrian's journeys.

MAKING CONNECTIONS

The following questions are intended to emphasize important ideas within the chapter.

1. Who were the winners and the losers in the creation of the republican empire? How did this create the circumstances that led to the century of crisis?

2. Between 133 B.C. and 44 B.C., what reforms of the republican government were attempted? How successful were they? Why did they succeed or fail?

3. In what way did Augustus modify the republican constitution to create the empire? What religious and social reforms did he impose?

4. What was the religious atmosphere of the Roman Empire? How did the Jews fit into the Roman political scheme? How did Christianity spread beyond Palestine? What was the system of authority within Christianity?

5. What does Hadrian's tour of his empire tell about the homogeneity of Roman culture? What does it tell us about the problems of maintaining the empire?

PUTTING LARGER CONCEPTS TOGETHER

The following questions test your ability to summarize the major conclusions of the chapter.

1. Consider the reasons for the collapse of the republic. How did the Roman Empire attempt to overcome these problems? What was different about the empire? What price was paid in order to make the empire successful?

2. Consider the nature of religion within the Roman republic. How did the rise of Christianity alter the culture of the Roman Empire?

SELF-TEST OF FACTUAL INFORMATION

1. In the first century B.C. slaves comprised what proportion of the total population of the Roman territories?

    a. one half
    b. one third
    c. one fourth
    d. one tenth

2. What two brothers, both of whom served as tribune, unsettled the political conditions of the late republic by proposing land reform?

    a. the Gracchi
    b. the Marii
    c. the Scipios
    d. the Taciti

3. When Pompey's supporters in the Roman Senate ordered Julius Caesar to return to Rome in 49 B.C., he

    a. launched the invasion of Britain.
    b. left his forces in Gaul to pursue his career in the Senate.
    c. refused to leave Gaul.
    d. returned to Rome with his legions and initiated a civil war.

4. Which of the following was *not* an action of Julius Caesar after defeating Pompey?

    a. increasing the membership of the Senate
    b. restoration of the republic
    c. settling veterans in colonies
    d. increasing the number of magistracies

5. What Roman poet of the late republic presented Epicureanism as an alternative to the hunger for power?

    a. Cicero
    b. Sallust
    c. Lucretius
    d. Marcus Aurelius

6. In order to restore the traditional values of the Roman republic, Augustus did all of the following *except*

    a. attempt to reinvigorate Roman religion by reviving ancient Roman cults.
    b. reconstruct the family unit by recreating the authority of the *paterfamilias*.
    c. patronize literary figures who shared his conservative views.
    d. surrender the authority of the principate and return to the republican constitution.

7. Which of the following emperors was not a member of the Flavian dynasty?

    a. Domitian
    b. Vespasian
    c. Nero
    d. Titus

8. Which of the following Jewish groups was willing to work with Rome and even accept some elements of Hellenism?

    a. Sadducees
    b. Hasidim
    c. Pharisees
    d. Zealots

9. Some emperors persecuted the Christians because, unlike many of the Jews, Christians

    a. wanted violent overthrow of the empire.
    b. rigidly excluded all Roman citizens from membership in their cult.
    c. refused to participate in the cult of the deified emperors.
    d. refused to pay taxes.

10. Epictetus and Marcus Aurelius espoused what philosophy?

    a. Epicureanism
    b. Stoicism
    c. Neoplatonism
    d. Christianity

Chapter 6

The Transformation of the Classical World

OUTLINE

I.   A Bride's Trousseau

The silver chest, probably part of a late imperial bride's trousseau, ties together the various strands of late Roman imperial culture. The pagan themes typical of an older Roman culture are joined with a clearly Christian injunction to "live in Christ." By the later empire, Christianity had evolved from a persecuted sect to the established state religion. To the cultural amalgam of the later Roman Empire were added the barbarian Germanic tribesmen, many of whom had, themselves, been converted to Christianity.

II.   The Crisis of the Third Century

A.   Introduction

By the third century, the Roman Empire was overextended. Its military defenses were inadequate to patrol the far-flung borders. The Roman economy also was near collapse. Tied to agriculture, the Romans had never developed commercial expertise. The shortage of liquid capital left industry underdeveloped. The administration of the empire remained similarly crude. With no sense of public credit, the government fell back on unsound monetary policies. The failure to develop a principle of succession also continued to plague the empire.

B.   Enrich the Army and Scorn the Rest

During the third century, the emperors failed militarily. When the rulers suffered defeat, the legions raised their own commanders as successors. Successful soldiers, regardless of their social status, could achieve the imperial purple, at least temporarily. These commanders, in turn, passed legislation in favor of the armies in order to maintain their newly won positions. Bribery of the military consisted of increased pay funded by debased coinage. As the quality of coinage declined, prices soared setting off new demands for pay increases and subsequent military revolutions. Most of the soldier/emperors were assassinated. As political instability increased, the empire was subject to more intense assaults from outside its borders.

C.   An Empire on the Defensive

The imperial administration was unable to deal effectively with widespread barbarian assaults on the borders. Some regional commanders chose to create independent, separatist governments. Political and military instability had devastating effects on the social organization of the empire. As before, a huge gulf arose between the *honestiores*—soldiers, senators, and those exempt from taxation—and the *humiliores*—the masses of the population on whom the tax burden of supporting the military fell. Despairing of survival, many men were driven to banditry. Such popular resistance to the imperial administration further disrupted political order.

D.   The Barbarian World

The attacks on the northern borders of the empire came from various peoples called Germans. Between the second and the fifth century, German political organization changed from typically small bands of kin to powerful tribal confederations. The basic social units of the Germans were households grouped together into related kindred units or clans. Clans were loosely grouped together in tribes. Fragmentation of tribal groups was common because of the feud, carried out against other kinship groups for any offense. Relationships between different clans were usually typified by raiding and pillaging. Tribal leaders attempted to create group solidarity by religious cults and the *comitatus*, the society of warriors. The *comitatus* sometimes served as the basis on which new tribal configurations could be formed. Intertribal violence produced a rough equilibrium of power that prevented the creation of unified Germanic political groups. Commercial and cultural interaction with the Roman empire destroyed Germanic equilibrium and initiated the development of larger Germanic political units. *Comitatus* commanders began to serve within the Roman armies and were favored with Roman wealth. Thus the Germanic military organization began to prevail over the original tribal society. The war band leader emerged as the political center around which new and more powerful confederations could coalesce. The increasing organization of Germanic peoples resulted in the Marcomannian Wars at the end of the second century and the confederation of Gothic peoples sufficiently powerful to challenge Roman authority.

III.   The Empire Restored

A.   Introduction

The emperors Aurelian and Diocletian temporarily halted the disintegration of the Roman empire.

B.   Diocletian, the God-Emperor

Diocletian maintained the lofty status of god-emperor, but recognized that the empire was too large for one man to administer. He created the tetrarchy, a division of the empire into four parts ruled by two emperors and two assistants called caesars. The division of the empire into eastern and western halves proved a durable reform. Diocletian also increased the number of provinces and the legions of bureaucrats to staff the new units. He tried to control rampant inflation by issuing new coinage and establishing price and wage controls. In order to shift the economic burden, the emperor imposed a new system of taxation. The key to his success was his control of the military and his separation of the army from administration. Some of Diocletian's reforms, though well-intentioned, failed. Attempts to control inflation and to maintain a stable currency fell through. Tax reforms bound small farmers to their land. Local administration also suffered, as the city council members were financially ruined. Failure of the Christians to support the cult of the deified emperor led to renewed persecution.

C.   Constantine, the Emperor of God

In 305 Diocletian resigned his position in favor of his assistant emperor. Instead of the anticipated orderly succession, a civil war ensued. Constantine, the winner, was the son of one of Diocletian's caesars. Constantine was converted to Christianity, a religion that now gained the acceptance of the state. Constantine also shifted his capital from Rome to the East. A new center, Constantinople, replaced the old capital as the focus of a Christian empire. Although Constantine preserved the old public religions during his own lifetime, his successors raised Christianity to the status of state religion. Bishops began to operate as magistrates within the Christian community, and the emperor sought to establish himself as head of Christendom. Constantine called the first great Church council at Nicaea and determined a major doctrinal controversy, the condemnation of Arianism. The acceptance of the state hastened the growth of Christianity within the Roman empire. By the fourth century, the number of Christians rose to thirty million.

IV.   Imperial Christianity

A.   Introduction

The Christian Church of the later Roman empire was well organized under the leadership of the bishops, but the Church remained divided by significant differences in theological interpretation. Two of the most important issues were the nature of Christ and the means by which salvation could be earned.

B.   Divinity, Humanity, and Salvation

The nature of the Trinity—Yahweh, Christ, and the Spirit—was a matter of debate among various Christian communities attempting to accommodate Christianity with the intellectual milieu of the later Roman empire. In particular the relationship between the divinity and humanity of Christ was problematic. Extreme positions described Christ as either entirely a creature or entirely divine. The first Christian theologian to explore the relations within the Trinity fully was Origen of Alexandria. He insisted on the divinity of Christ, but seemed to relegate him to a lesser divinity than the Father. The question of the divinity of Christ had to be adjudicated by Constantine at Nicaea in 325. Controversies continued to rage, even after Nicaea. Arians, who believed that Christ was not equal with the Father, successfully converted the Goths to their cause. Monophysites, who argued that Christ was only divine with no human attributes, gained adherents in Syria and Egypt. A council at Chalcedon in 451 proclaimed that not only did the Trinity consist of three divinities, but also that Christ possessed both a fully human and a fully divine nature. This position was never accepted in regions of the East where Monophysitism continued to flourish. In the western half of the empire, theologians concentrated more on defining the process of salvation. Donatists and Pelagians argued that only a select few capable of practicing more perfect lives could be assured of salvation. Donatists wished to cast out of the Church all those who, in times of persecution, had collaborated with the Roman government. Pelagians taught that humans could resist sin and achieve salvation without Christ's sacrifice. The primary opponent of these elitist theologies was Augustine, bishop of Hippo in North Africa. In responding to Donatists and Pelagians, Augustine provided a foundation for the Christian's relationship to God. Augustine posited a "city of God" that superseded all earthly governments. One participated in the true "city" through the sacraments. Salvation was a gift of grace granted freely by God to the elect. Thus a distinction was made between the visible Church that existed in the material world and the invisible Church of the elect. Christianity was not dependent on the survival of Rome or Roman culture, for the invisible Church was unaffected by the political storms of the later empire.

C.   The Call of the Desert

Some Christians chose to abandon society entirely in search of a more purely contemplative life. An Egyptian peasant, Anthony (250–355), gave away all his earthly possessions and retreated to the desert where he began to attract other Christians seeking to cut themselves off from the secular world.

D.   Monastic Communities

Those who chose to abandon the secular world followed two paths: communal organization or solitary life. Communal monastic living first became popular in Egypt. There communities of Christians dedicated themselves to rigorous prayer and self-mortification under the complete command of abbots who ruled the communities. The fame of these communities as models of Christian living and contemplation spread throughout the Roman empire. The Egyptian monasteries attracted many recruits, including Jerome who founded a monastery in Palestine. There he translated the Bible into Latin. Basil the Great transferred the Egyptian model of communal living to the Greek-speaking world. Basil was more connected to the secular world of politics than the abbots of Egypt, and the Greek monasteries became the training centers for the non-monastic heads of the Church in the eastern half of the Roman empire. Basil, himself, became bishop of Caesarea. Benedict of Nursia created the most popular model of monasticism in the West. Benedict's rule enjoined monks to a life of poverty, chastity, and obedience. The rule divided the day into regular intervals of prayer and meditation. Unlike the East, western monks and abbots generally remained aloof from secular politics.

E.   Solitaries and Hermits

The alternative to communal living was isolation. This practice was most common in the Syrian desert where hermits lived lives of nomadic individualism. These Christian radicals rejected ancient society in entirety. One hermit, Simeon Stylites, supposedly lived for more than thirty years on the top of a pillar. Because the rest of Christian society tended to view the hermits as supermen and women, these spiritual athletes were called upon for advice and as arbitrators of social ills. The tradition of holy hermits was not common in the western half of the Roman empire.

V.   A Parting of the Ways

A.   Introduction

The appearance of the Huns from the East shattered the Gothic confederation on the borders of the Roman empire. The Visigoths, the largest of the Germanic groups, sought refuge in the empire. Relations between the Romans and Germans soon deteriorated. At the battle of Adrianople, the Visigoths defeated and killed the emperor Valens. In the aftermath of their victory, the Visigoths were permitted to reside in the empire under their own government as an independent people. From their original entry point in the eastern half of the empire, the Visigoths migrated under the leadership of their kings to the West. They entered Italy and took Rome in A.D. 410. From Italy they passed on to southern France and Spain.

B.   The Barbarization of the West

The armies of the empire were Germanic long before the Visigothic invasion. The Visigoths were simply seen as a new form of Germanic "army" and were supported by the diversion of tax revenues from the regions in which they settled. The Visigothic kings established the kingdom of Toulouse in southern France with imperial consent. Similarly, the Vandals established their kingdom in northern Africa. From this Mediterranean base, the Vandals attacked Roman shipping and Rome itself. With the disintegration of the Hunnic confederacy in 451, the Ostrogoths regained their independence. They entered the eastern half of the Roman empire, but were sent to Italy by the eastern emperor, Zeno. Under the command of their king, Theodoric, the Ostrogoths established a kingdom in Italy. As the last emperor in the West had been set aside in A.D. 476, the Romans regarded Theodoric as the supreme military commander of that half of the empire. The last vestiges of Roman military command were represented by the armies of Flavius Aetius and Syagrius in Gaul. These commanders represented the interests of the local Gallo-Roman aristocracy. The Franks swept away this last bastion of Romanism. Britain was also abandoned to Germanic invasion. During the fifth century, clans of Germans known as Anglo-Saxons swept the Celtic population of the island to the west and north. The emperors continued to preserve the fiction that the Germanic kingdoms were Roman armies in the employ of the empire. Provincial elites accepted the barbarians, because they were able to carve out huge estates as autonomous lordships without the interference of the imperial government. The only disagreement between barbarians and provincial elites was over religion. The Visigoths and Ostrogoths had been converted to Arianism, a condemned form of Christianity. The orthodox residents of the western half of the empire viewed the Germans as heretics. In the absence of imperial administration in the western half of the empire, the Christian episcopacy began to function as the local authority. The office of bishop was increasingly identified with the local Gallo-Roman aristocracy.

C.   The Hellenization of the East

Unlike the West, the East avoided the process of Germanization. The East fell back on Hellenistic traditions that antedated the Roman empire. Tax structures remained relatively undisturbed, and the barbarians were never able to gain a stranglehold on the military or the administration. Similarly, the Church did not replace the imperial administration.

TIMELINE

Insert the following events into the timeline. This should help you to compare important historical events chronologically.

Visigothic sack of Rome
beginning of reign of Diocletian
battle of Adrianople

Theodoric's invasion of Italy
Council of Chalcedon
Council of Nicaea

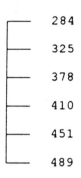

284

325

378

410

451

489

TERMS, PEOPLE, EVENTS

The following terms, people, and events are important to your understanding of the chapter. Define each one.

honestiores	*humiliores*	*wergeld*
comitatus	Diocletian	Constantine
tetrarchy	Mulvian Bridge	Council of Nicaea
Huns	Attila	Gothic confederation
Visigoths	Alaric	Vandals
Theodoric	Arianism	Christological controversy
Origen	Augustine	Council of Chalcedon
Donatists	Pelagians	Monophysites
Anthony	Basil the Great	Benedict of Nursia

MAP EXERCISE

The following exercise is intended to clarify the geophysical environment and the spatial relationships among the important objects and places mentioned in the chapter. Locate the following places on the map.

boundaries of eastern and western halves of empire

Rome   Constantinople   Jerusalem
Alexandria   Nicaea

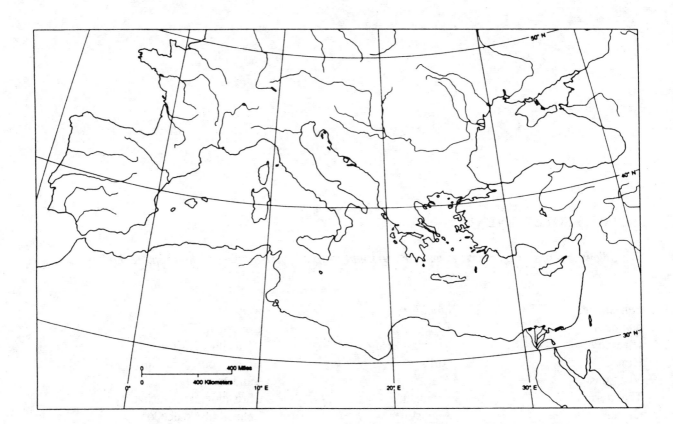

1.   Diocletian's division of the empire led to two significantly different cultures. Which half of the empire was more heavily Hellenized? In which half did early forms of monasticism and the earliest doctrinal controversies first appear? In which half were the first Germanic kingdoms established?

MAKING CONNECTIONS

The following questions are intended to emphasize important ideas within the chapter.

1. What were the internal and external causes of the third century crisis for the Roman empire?

2. Discuss the social and political organization of the Germanic peoples.

3. Through what reforms did Diocletian restore the empire? Were all the reforms effective?

4. What impact did Constantine's acceptance of Christianity have on the Roman empire?

5. Discuss the nature of the Christological controversy. What was the contribution of Augustine?

6. What was monasticism? Discuss its origins.

7. What Germanic tribes successfully invaded the Roman empire following the fourth century AD.? Where did they establish kingdoms? What was their relationship with the local Gallo-Roman elites?

8. Why did the eastern half of the Roman empire escape the establishment of Germanic kingdoms?

PUTTING LARGER CONCEPTS TOGETHER

The following questions test your ability to summarize the major conclusions of the chapter.

1. Is it accurate to say that the Roman empire fell? How would it be necessary to modify that statement? What date would you pick for the fall of the Roman empire?

2. What was the impact of Christianity on the Roman empire? How did the various theological controversies help to establish Christianity within the system of authority of the Roman empire? What was the relationship of Christianity to the Germanic tribesmen?

SELF-TEST OF FACTUAL INFORMATION

1. Which of the following was *not* a significant problem of the later Roman Empire?

   a. lead-lined aqueducts that poisoned the population
   b. an economic system that did not serve the needs of Rome
   c. the sheer size of the empire
   d. an inequitable tax system that was not able to tap the wealth of the aristocracy

2. Which of the following was *not* typical of early Germanic society?

   a. strong, centralized states
   b. *wergeld*
   c. the *comitatus*
   d. shared myths of common ancestry

3. Which of the following was *not* a reform for which Diocletian was responsible?

   a. the reduction of the bureaucracy of imperial administration
   b. the division of the Roman empire into eastern and western parts
   c. the elevation of the status of emperor to both *dominus* and *Iovius*
   d. the militarization of Roman society to prepare the empire for victory

4. Which of the following statements concerning Constantine is most accurate?

   a. During his reign the Visigoths swept across the western half of the empire.
   b. He was responsible for the growth of Christianity from a persecuted minority to a favored cult.
   c. Paganism was rapidly disestablished during his reign.
   d. Constantine was the last emperor to persecute Christians actively.

5. The concept of the "City of God" was developed by what theologian?

   a. Plotinus
   b. Origen
   c. Benedict of Nursia
   d. Augustine

6. Who was responsible for providing the definitive form of monasticism in the Greek-speaking world of Christianity?

   a. Anthony
   b. Basil the Great
   c. Pachomius
   d. Benedict of Nursia

7. What Germanic tribe defeated the eastern Roman emperor Valens at Adrianople?

    a. Visigoths
    b. Ostrogoths
    c. Vandals
    d. Franks

8. Which of the following statements is *not* accurate?

    a. By the fifth century barbarians made up the bulk of the Roman army.
    b. Commanders in the later imperial Roman armies were often barbarians.
    c. Barbarian commanders were notoriously disloyal to Rome.
    d. Later emperors accepted whole barbarian peoples and settled them within the empire.

9. The aristocracy of the western half of the Roman empire

    a. withered away with the disappearance of the imperial government.
    b. welcomed the disappearance of the imperial government in the sense that it meant an end to taxation and the jurisdiction of public officials.
    c. were most often pagan and opposed the appearance of Church authority.
    d. lost control of the local administration to Germanic kings.

10. In contrast to the western half of the empire, the East

    a. rapidly declined and then disintegrated completely.
    b. managed to survive and prosper.
    c. slowly faded into the Dark Ages.
    d. fragmented into many small kingdoms dominated by barbarian lords.

Chapter 7

The Classical Legacy in the East: Byzantium and Islam

OUTLINE

I. From Temple to Mosque

The Great Mosque of Damascus represented the cultural amalgamation that had taken place in parts of what had once been the eastern half of the Roman Empire. Built on the remains of what had once been a temple to the pagan gods—to the Syriac Hadad, and then to Jupiter, the patriarch of the Roman pantheon—a Christian Church dedicated to Saint John the Baptist represented the conversion of the Empire to Christianity. Following the fall of Damascus to the Muslim forces, the Church of St. John was converted to an Islamic mosque. One of the sacred relics associated with the old church was retained in the midst of the abstract symbolism of Islam.

II. The Byzantines

A. Introduction

Although the eastern half of the Roman empire did not fall to Germanic tribes, it had severe problems. Political factions—the Blues and Greens—associated with rival parties in the Hippodrome created instability in the capital. The population of the eastern empire was divided into many ethnic groups, some of which were scarcely less barbaric than the Germans. The urban centers of the East began to decline in favor of the agricultural countryside. Finally, the great metropolitan bishops of Christianity constantly squabbled over political supremacy and the questions of orthodoxy.

B. Justinian and the Creation of the Byzantine State

The emperor Justinian temporarily restored the fortunes of the Byzantine state. Justinian mounted a great reconquest of some parts of the empire lost to the Germanic tribes. The generals Belisarius and Narses took back northern Africa from the Vandals, Italy from the Ostrogoths, and a part of Spain from the Visigoths. The army was also used to suppress the factions in the circus. The enormous expense of Justinian's ambitious military policy was passed on in taxes to the residents of the empire. Justinian is also credited with codifying the Roman legal system, and his code has provided the model for many European legal systems. The magnificence of Justinian's achievements were matched by the strain on the treasury. Bankrupt successors were unable to deal with renewed assaults on the borders of the empire. The Sassanid Empire, a successor state of the Seleucid Empire, captured Egypt, Palestine, and Syria. The emperor Heraclius recaptured the eastern territories from the Sassanids, but the weakened Byzantine state could not defend its easternmost regions from the Muslims indefinitely.

C.   Emperors and Individuals

Byzantine society was characterized by the direct relationship between an all-powerful emperor and citizens of all ranks. The emperor, sometimes assisted or even replaced by his spouse, was the sole source of authority in Byzantium. All other members of Byzantine society venerated the emperor in the eastern tradition. An enormous bureaucracy carried out the actual tasks of administration. After Justinian, the empire was divided into about twenty-five military districts or themes. Soldier/citizens within the themes received land in return for military service. The success of the civil and military administration left no room for the establishment of aristocratic political elites. Social organization devolved to the level of the nuclear family. In the countryside, the highest level of political organization was the village. Even agricultural organization was based on the household rather than on cooperative communal effort. Mountainous geography contributed to regional isolation. Of the cities, Constantinople dwarfed the others in population and as a commercial center. The empire's cities were industrial centers, particularly as producers of silk.

D.   A Foretaste of Heaven

The common denominator of Byzantine culture was Orthodox Christianity. After the rise of Islam in the seventh century, the divisive squabbles among metropolitan bishoprics came to an end as Antioch, Alexandria, and Jerusalem fell under the rule of the caliphs. In the Byzantine empire, the patriarch of Constantinople assumed primacy in the Orthodox Church. The emperors, also resident in Constantinople, appointed and dismissed patriarchs at will and were the true heads of the Church. The liturgy of Eastern Orthodoxy came to reflect the political order of Byzantium. The monasteries retained their political independence against the interests of the episcopacy and the emperor. Icons, religious images thought to have mystic powers as intermediaries of the saints, strengthened the religious appeal of the monks. Beginning with Emperor Leo III, emperors sought to suppress the worship of icons. The attack on the images, iconoclasm, was a thinly veiled assault on monastic independence. Persecution of those who kept icons, iconodules, was carried out systematically until the end of the eighth century and then sporadically until the middle of the ninth century. Renewed acceptance of icons after 843 restored the influence of the monasteries.

III.   The Rise of Islam

A.   Introduction

Islam incorporated elements of Judaism and traditional Arabic worship. Similarly, Muslim society merged Arab, Roman, Hellenistic, Persian, and Jewish societies.

B.   Arabia Before the Prophet

Arabia existed until the seventh century on the borders of the Byzantine and Sassanid empires. The Bedouin nomads of the Arabian deserts were, like the Germanic tribes before entry into the Roman empire, organized in kinship groups and depended on the feud to settle disputes. Authority, such as it was, was limited to kinship heads. The kinship groups supported themselves by herding, commerce, and raiding. Goods were held in common by all members of the kindred. Although there were some Christians and Jews among the Arab tribesmen, most Arabs were pagans who worshipped various tribal deities. Sanctuaries, *haram*, where feuding was forbidden grew up around designated holy sites. One of these sanctuaries was located in the city of Mecca where the Quraysh tribe guarded the

Ka`bah, a sacred black rock. With its neutrality guaranteed, Mecca grew into a major trade center for all Arabs, although the Quraysh regulated the commerce.

C.   Muhammad, Prophet of God

Muhammad was born a member of a less distinguished family of the Quraysh. He made a successful marriage to Khadijah, a wealthy widow, and entered the ranks of the Quraysh merchants of Mecca. In 610 Muhammad received his first revelation that he was Allah's messenger. His complete revelations were recorded in the *Qur'an* (Koran). Muhammad began to carry his message to the Arabs of Mecca. The governing elite not only refused his message, but became increasingly hostile to Muhammad's insistence on obedience to the word of Allah as it appeared in the *Qur'an.* In 622 Muhammad abandoned Mecca for Medina, a smaller trading city that called on him to help the Medinans end civil strife. The emigration to Medina, called the *Hijra,* marks the beginning of the Islamic calendar. At Medina, Muhammad united the Arabs in a new religious community, the *Umma,* that superseded tribal and clan affiliations. The Jewish clans and all those who refused to recognize Muhammad's leadership were expelled in the name of Allah. With Medina consolidated under his command, Muhammad moved against the Quraysh of Mecca. First he destroyed the Meccan trade network, then took the city itself in 629. From Medina and Mecca, the message of Islam spread rapidly throughout the Arabic tribes. Believers were attracted to the new religion through vivid descriptions of the delights of heaven and the pains of hell. There were also economic incentives. Mecca, its *Ka`bah* converted to an Islamic sanctuary, regained its centrality in Arabian trade, and the Quraysh rushed to accept Allah as the sole god. Converts to Islam were permitted to participate in the holy wars that forcibly brought other tribes into the *Umma.*

D.   The Spread of Islam

Muhammad's death in 632 disrupted the solidarity of the *Umma.* The Prophet had established no order of succession after his death, and disputes over political leadership arose between his immediate family, his earliest converts, and the traditional leading clans of the Quraysh in Mecca. In addition, many tribes felt only a personal loyalty to Muhammad, not to his successors. To maintain the *Umma* the orthodox caliphs, Muhammad's immediate successors, called for a holy war against tribes that had recanted their faith in Islam. Muslim armies gained control of all of Arabia, then extended their campaign to conquests of the neighboring Sassanid and Byzantine empires. Internal disruption within the Byzantine empire, particularly over religious disputes, paved the way for the Islamic invasion. Many Christians and Jews in Syria, Palestine, Egypt, and northern Africa viewed the Muslims as liberators from Byzantine impiety. Islamic armies reached the outer walls of Constantinople on two occasions.

E.   Authority and Government in Islam

The creation of an Islamic empire created enormous constitutional difficulty for the Arabs. The *Qur'an* was silent on secular government. Two opposing traditions of government arose. In the first model, the *Umma* represented simply a new type of tribe, subject to traditional patterns of secular leadership provided by tribal leaders such as the Quraysh. The second model was more rigorously religious in outlook. According to the second view, only a member of Muhammad's immediate family had sufficient moral purity to direct the affairs of the *Umma.* The Arabs initially left the administrative and economic networks untouched. Elites continued to govern without disruption. Only state property was confiscated for the *Umma.* Private property was largely undisturbed.

Unequal division of the spoils of conquest caused dissatisfaction with the orthodox caliphate. The disagreement created a serious division between those who favored an immediate relative of the Prophet—represented by 'Ali, Muhammad's nephew—and those who desired continued government by major clan leaders. Although 'Ali was named caliph, relatives of Uthman in the Umayyad clan who commanded the military in Syria refused to recognize 'Ali. In 661 the Umayyads killed 'Ali and established a caliphate with a new capital at Damascus in the Umayyad stronghold of Syria. 'Ali's partisans refused to recognize the purity of the Umayyad claim to authority and founded an opposition party, Shi'ism. The Umayyads tried to convert the Islamic conquests into a secular state. The Umayyad caliphs extended the territories of Islam to the walls of Constantinople, the borders of China, and along the southern coast of the Mediterranean to Spain. The Umayyads attempted to maintain a strictly Arab elite within their state. As the number of non-Arab converts to Islam grew, dissatisfaction with the concept of Arab—especially Quraysh—dominance festered. Demands for greater equality among all Muslims coalesced with reformers' claims into a broad movement that unseated the Umayyads. Distant relatives of Muhammad, the 'Abbasids, were recognized as rightful successors. In 750 the 'Abbasids replaced the Umayyads as rulers everywhere but in Spain. At the outset, the 'Abbasids represented the reform movement and set out to govern according to strict religious principles. Arabs lost their control of Islamic government which was opened to all Muslims. The 'Abbasids created a new capital in Baghdad, a recognition of the new importance of Iraq and Persia in the new government. The 'Abbasids claimed absolute rights of government based on the righteousness of their claims to power. The caliphs created a centralized bureaucracy on the model of the eastern empires. Slave soldiers replaced the originally Arab armies. By the tenth century, the 'Abbasid caliphs lost absolute control over Islam. Local military commanders, *emirs,* took over provincial governments. Various Shi'ite movements successfully established separatist governments. The most important Shi'ite revolution resulted in the creation of the Fatimid caliphate in Egypt. A third caliphate arose in Spain under 'Abd ar-Rahman III. External invasion led to the final collapse of the 'Abbasids. Seljuk Turks conquered Baghdad in 1055, while much of northern Africa fell to Moroccan Berbers. The invasions disrupted the commercial and economic systems of the Islamic empire.

F.   Islamic Civilization

The Islamic conquest, far from destroying the conquered territories, at first brought about agricultural recovery and commercial revival. Unlike the Germanic invaders of the western half of the Roman empire, the Arabs avidly adopted the culture of Byzantium and Persia. Persian, Hellenistic, and Roman works of science, mathematics, and medicine were discovered and expanded. In philosophy, the Arabs translated the works of both Plato and Aristotle. Arab commentators such as Ya'qub al-Kindi, Ibn Sina, and Ibn Rushd sought to accommodate Greek philosophy to Islamic theology. The Arabs thus became the conservators of much of ancient culture lost in the Germanic West.

IV.   The Byzantine Apogee and Decline, 1000–1453

A.   Introduction

In the tenth and eleventh centuries, the Byzantine empire was able to regain temporarily its ascendancy in the eastern Mediterranean. Armies of the Macedonian dynasty regained footholds in Italy, Syria, and Asia Minor. Missions from the Orthodox Church carried Byzantine religion and culture to the Balkans and to Russia from there. Military successes brought with them a brief economic and cultural rebirth as well. Byzantine literature, in the main, remained fixed on Hellenistic models.

B.   The Disintegration of the empire

After the Macedonian dynasty, serious problems once again threatened the Byzantine empire. Foremost among the difficulties was the increasing dominance of the aristocratic elite in control of both real property and the military. As the aristocracy began to intervene between the imperial administration and the peasantry, they became sufficiently powerful to initiate revolts against the government in Constantinople. At about the same time, foreign merchants, particularly Italians, began to monopolize Byzantine commerce to the detriment of the state's finances. Finally, the empire faced more serious threats of foreign invasion. The Normans of southern Italy, under Robert Guiscard, menaced the western frontiers, while the forces of the Seljuk Turks invaded Asia Minor. In 1071 the Turks defeated the Byzantines and captured the emperor at the battle of Manzikert.

C.   The Conquests of Constantinople and Baghdad

The Comnenian dynasty of Byzantium temporarily halted the decay within the empire by aligning itself with the aristocracy. External threats, however, remained serious. From the West, both the Normans and the bishop of Rome presented challenges to Byzantine supremacy. In 1054 a formal break between the obediences of the Orthodox Church and the Roman Church occurred. Following Manzikert, the Comneni were willing to embrace an alliance with the military powers of the West in order to stem the advance of the Turks. In response to Byzantine requests, the bishop of Rome called the First Crusade. Reckless freebooters entered the empire on the way to the Holy Land. By 1099 the crusaders successfully established the Latin kingdom of Jerusalem. At first overjoyed, the Byzantines came to fear the growing presence of westerners in the East. In 1204 Byzantine fears were realized when a "crusade" actually captured Constantinople. Although a Byzantine emperor was crowned again in 1261, the empire was fatally weakened. Like Byzantium, the 'Abbasid empire fell to external invaders. In 1221 the Mongols from the steppes of Asia under the leadership of Genghis Khan smashed the remnants of Islamic unity. In 1258 Baghdad fell to the horde, and the last 'Abbasid caliph was executed. The Mongols disrupted the disorganized Seljuk territories before faltering before the defenses of Egypt. When the Mongols withdrew, one of the Seljuk principalities, the Ottomans, began to overwhelm its neighbors. In the middle of the fifteenth century, Constantinople finally fell to the invaders.

TIMELINE

Insert the following events into the timeline. This should help you to compare important historical events chronologically.

fall of Baghdad to Mongols
'Abbasids overthrow Umayyads
fall of Constantinople

Muhammad's initial revelation
Muhammad's flight from Mecca
Schism splits churches of Rome and Constantinople

—	610
—	622
—	750
—	1054
—	1258
—	1453

TERMS, PEOPLE, EVENTS

The following terms, people, and events are important to your understanding of the chapter. Define each one.

Byzantine empire	Justinian	Theodora
Justinian Code	themes	eunuchs
patriarch	iconoclasts	iconodules
Islam	Muhammad	*haram*
Ka'bah	*Qur'an* (Koran)	*Hijra*
Umma	*jihad*	'Ali
Quraysh	Umayyads	'Abbasids
sunnah	*hadith*	'Ubayd Allah the Fatimid
Ya'qub al-Kindi	Ibn Sina	Ibn Rushd
Macedonian dynasty	*pronoia*	Comnenian dynasty
Manzikert	Seljuk Turks	Ottoman Turks

MAP EXERCISE

The following exercise is intended to clarify the geophysical environment and the spatial relationships among the important objects and places mentioned in the chapter. Locate the following places on the map.

Constantinople   Mecca   Medina
Damascus   Baghdad
Draw the boundaries of the original Byzantine Empire

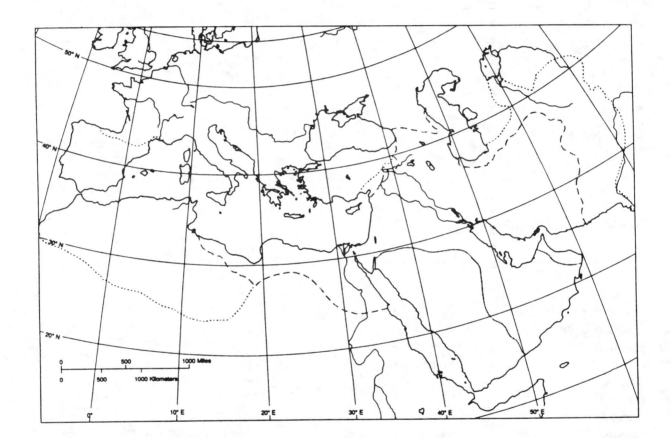

1.   Byzantium contracted while Islam expanded. What territories were lost to Byzantium as a result of the initial Islamic expansion in the seventh century?

2.   Starting with Mecca, draw an arrow to each of the succeeding capitals of Islam. In what direction was the "center" of Islam moving?

MAKING CONNECTIONS

The following questions are intended to emphasize important ideas within the chapter.

1. What were the inherent difficulties in maintaining unity in the Byzantine empire? How did religious differences (including iconoclasm) contribute to disunity?

2. What was the administration of the Byzantine Empire?

3. What was the nature of social organization in pre-Islamic Arabia? Why was Mecca important?

4. How did Muhammad's concept of the *Umma* contribute to political unification of Arabs?

5. Why did the Muslims experience difficulty in agreeing on a principle of governing the *Umma*? What alternatives were proposed? Which alternative was represented by the Umayyads? Which alternative was represented by the 'Abbasids?

6. What was the relationship of the Arabs to Hellenistic culture?

7. What internal and external problems led to the collapse of the Byzantine empire? What internal and external problems led to the collapse of the 'Abbasid dynasty?

PUTTING LARGER CONCEPTS TOGETHER

The following questions test your ability to summarize the major conclusions of the chapter.

1. To what extent can it be said that Islamic expansion was predicated on trade? What important concept would be missing from this analysis?

2. Compare the role and function of Christianity within the Roman empire to the role and function of Islam within the 'Abbasid empire? See Chapter 6.

SELF-TEST OF FACTUAL INFORMATION

1. Which of the following was *not* a cause of divisiveness in the Byzantine empire?

    a. rival political factions' association with Hippodrome teams
    b. ethnic differences among the population
    c. religious squabbles among the metropolitan bishops
    d. permanent conquest by German tribes

2. Which of the following best describes the role of the senate in the Byzantine empire?

    a. wasted away, window dressing to the imperial cult
    b. reformed, a powerful part of the Byzantine constitution
    c. an aristocratic oligarchy, it replaced imperial authority
    d. abolished

3. Which of the following statements most accurately describes Byzantine monasticism?

    a. The monasteries were absolutely dependent on the favor of the emperors.
    b. The monasteries sought to eliminate the veneration of icons.
    c. The religious appeal of the monasteries was often based on icons.
    d. Monasteries played an insignificant part in Byzantine culture.

4. Who was responsible for the restoration of icon veneration?

    a. Theodora
    b. Leo III
    c. Justinian
    d. Heraclius

5. Mecca's importance in pre-Islamic Arabia was due to its status as

    a. a major seaport.
    b. *haram*, a religious sanctuary.
    c. the capital of the Roman province of Arabia.
    d. the only city in the Arabian peninsula.

6. According to Islamic orthodoxy, which of the following statements best describes the *Qu'ran*?

    a. It is an exact and complete revelation without need for interpretation.
    b. Like the Bible, it requires considerable theological explanation.
    c. It was the work of a dedicated group of Muhammad's followers.
    d. It was discovered written on hidden gold tablets.

7. The models of administration in the Islamic empire were drawn from

    a. the *Qur'an*.
    b. the *hadith* concerning Muhammad's life.
    c. Arabic society.
    d. Byzantine and Sassanid bureaucracy and government.

8. Belief that the legitimate leadership of Islam could only come from the house of 'Ali created the religious and political sect called

    a. Kharij.
    b. Sunnites.
    c. Shi'ites.
    d. Sufi.

9. What dynasty came to power in 750 following the overthrow of the Umayyads?

    a. Ottomans
    b. 'Abbasids
    c. orthodox caliphs
    d. Fatimids

10. What was the impact of the Arab conquests on the Hellenistic cultures of the East?

    a. As desert conquerors, the Arabs destroyed Hellenistic culture.
    b. The Muslims found Hellenistic culture to be depraved and immoral.
    c. The Muslims became the protectors and preservers of Hellenistic culture.
    d. There was no impact, because the cultures remained entirely separate.

Chapter 8

The West in the Early Middle Ages, 500–900

OUTLINE

I. The Chapel at the Waters

The Germanic conquerors of the western half of the Roman Empire buttressed their claims to sovereignty with the superficial trappings of Roman culture. The greatest of the Germanic monarchs, Charlemagne of the Franks, built his residence at Aachen in the manner of a Roman palace. With his coronation as emperor in 800, Charlemagne took on the political mantle of the Roman Empire just as the capital at Aachen bound the architecture of a defeated culture to the purposes of a Germanic kingdom.

II. The Making of the Barbarian Kingdoms, 500–750

A. Introduction

Although the Roman Empire in the West seemed undisturbed after the deposition of the last emperor in 476, real power lay in the hands of Germanic kings and military commanders.

B. The Goths: From Success to Extinction

There were two Gothic kingdoms in the fifth century: the Ostrogothic kingdom of Italy and the Visigothic kingdom of Toulouse. Theodoric, king of the Ostrogoths, was the most successful Gothic monarch. He established a bipartite government in Italy that continued the Roman civil administration for the Gallo-Roman population and recognized Germanic kingship and military authority for the Goths. On Theodoric's death, civil disputes broke out among the Goths. Sensing the weakness of Germanic government, the Byzantine emperor Justinian ordered an invasion of Italy. After twenty years of warfare, the Goths were defeated and ceased to exist as an independent people. The Byzantines were able to hold only the southern parts of Italy. The northern half of Italy fell to a subsequent tribe of Germanic invaders, the Lombards. The bishops of Rome emerged as the most efficient protectors of the Gallo-Roman population. Tensions between Lombards and the Roman population eased when the Germans converted to orthodox Christianity. The Visigothic kingdom of Toulouse did not long survive the Ostrogothic kingdom of Italy. Defeated by the Franks in 507, the Visigothic kingdom became concentrated in Spain. Originally Arian, like the Ostrogoths, the Visigoths finally converted to orthodox Christianity in the mid-sixth century. Conversion allowed the use of the Spanish episcopacy as a governing council. Persecution of the large Jewish population and division between the kings and the aristocracy weakened the Visigothic kingdom by the eighth century. In 711 the Muslims easily overthrew the Visigothic kings and established an independent caliphate under the Umayyads.

C.   The Anglo-Saxons: From Pagan Conquerors to Christian Missionaries

The Germanic conquerors of Britain did not create a single kingdom, but organized themselves in small political units numbering as many as eleven kingdoms. Less exposed to Roman culture than the Goths, the Anglo-Saxons generally destroyed remnants of the ancient empire. Anglo-Saxon society consisted of free farmers dominated by petty kings and war-band leaders. The Anglo-Saxons were pagans at the time of their migration. Two groups of missionaries, Irish and Roman, were responsible for the conversion of the Germanic tribesmen. As the Irish and Roman churches differed in organization and calendar of religious observances, eventually their missionary efforts came into conflict. King Oswy of Northumbria decided the issue in 664 at the Synod of Whitby. The Bretwalda selected the more hierarchical Roman form of Christianity, thus tying the Anglo-Saxons to Rome and the Continent. Under the Roman church, Anglo-Saxon society became a source of scholars, artists, and missionaries. After the beginning of the eighth century, the Anglo-Saxons provided many of the missions to convert the heathen Germans of the continent of Europe.

D.   The Franks: An Enduring Legacy

Until the end of the fifth century, the Franks were a loosely organized client confederation of the Roman Empire. Their primary function was to supply soldiers for the Roman frontier defenses. In 486, the Frankish king Clovis began a series of military conquests, beginning with the elimination of Syagrius, the last Roman military commander in the West. Clovis' conversion to orthodox Christianity allowed him to ally himself with the Gallo-Roman aristocracy. The mixed force of Gallo-Romans and Franks eliminated most Germanic rivals. In short order, the Burgundians, Thuringians, Bavarians, and Visigoths fell before the Frankish advance. Clovis' dynasty, the Merovingians, lasted only until the mid-eighth century.

III.   Living in the New Europe

A.   Introduction

Although the establishment of the Germanic kingdoms caused few overt changes in the lives of inhabitants of the western half of the Roman Empire, a new society consisting of agricultural laborers and a combined Gallo-Roman/Germanic aristocracy emerged. Germanic and Roman political institutions slowly evolved into medieval kingship.

B.   Creating the European Peasantry

Slavery, commonplace in the Roman agricultural system, disappeared in the early Middle Ages. Previously servile families were moved to independent households. The social gulf between free and formerly servile agricultural laborers narrowed. Both groups formed the medieval peasantry, subject to the private justice of those who had authority over the land. With the division of agricultural labor into individual households responsible for cultivation of larger estates, the manse—the individual household unit—became the foundation of the agricultural economy. Heads of households, male or female, exercised authority over other members of the family group. The peasantry was largely a Christian population, unlike the agricultural laborers of the ancient world. By the sixth century, pagan rites had largely been transformed into Christian ones. By the ninth century, parish churches existed in almost every peasant village. Christianity and the Christian celebrations became an integral part of peasant society.

C.   Creating the European Aristocracy

The Germanic traditions of aristocracy depended on wealth derived from military service under the kings. Roman aristocracy derived its authority from its control of landed wealth. The Roman source of authority was inextricably bound up with Christianity. Many of the Gallo-Roman aristocrats were bishops themselves or related to the episcopacy. Aristocratic society highly prized the martial activities of hunting and warfare. Within the elite, women held a higher social status than in either Germanic or Roman society. The opening of religious life in monastic organizations to women broadened their opportunities for economic and political independence.

D.   Governing Europe

The aristocracy and the kings of early medieval kingdoms shared an uneasy partnership, normally limited to military ventures. During times of war, the kings' powers were absolute. At other times, his authority was strictly limited. Monarchs had no formal judicial authority other than as a voluntary court of appeal. Kings attempted to place themselves at the head of the remnants of the old Roman civil administration with mixed success. Better hope for authority stemmed from the kings' role as protectors of the Church, and many royal advisers were drawn from the ranks of the clergy. Kings had no fixed capitals, but wandered from one part of their kingdoms to another. Local authority in the king's absence was held by the aristocracy. Among the Franks, local representatives of the king were called *counts*. In Anglo-Saxon England, the royal appointees were called *ealdormen*. When kings were not vigilant, counts and ealdormen could become virtually independent lords within their territories.

IV.   The Carolingian Achievement

A.   Introduction

By the end of the seventh century, the Merovingian kings of the Franks had lost most of their authority to regional aristocrats, the most important of which was the family of Charles Martel, the Carolingians. From their positions as mayors of the palace of Austrasia, the Carolingians extended their authority over Neustria and Burgundy. Critical to the growth of Carolingian influence was their policy toward the Church. Loyal followers were rewarded with bishoprics and abbacies. More importantly, Charles Martel aligned himself closely with the bishop of Rome. The Carolingian alliance with the pope paid off in 751 when the papacy recognized Pippin III as king of the Franks in preference to the Merovingians. Royal legitimacy was thus based on ecclesiastical sanction.

B.   Charlemagne and the Renewal of the West

The greatest Carolingian was Pippin's son, Charlemagne. He engaged in a number of successful military ventures: conquest of the kingdom of the Lombards in Italy, incorporation of the Saxons, annexation of the buffer zone between the kingdom of the Franks and the Islamic caliphate in Spain, and the destruction of the Avars. The spoils of conquest were dedicated to cultural rejuvenation. Charlemagne established schools and recruited intellectuals to promote an educational renaissance. The Carolingians also sought to reform ecclesiastical institutions. The kings attempted to get all monasteries to conform to the Benedictine rule and to regularize the education of parish clergy. In order to finance ecclesiastical reforms, tithes—the ten percent tax on all Christians—became mandatory.

C.   Carolingian Government

To govern his vast kingdom, Charlemagne made use of counts. To curb the propensity of the counts toward independence, the king sent teams of emissaries, the *missi dominici,* to examine the government of each county. Churchmen were frequent members of the royal administration. Although crude in comparison to the Roman Empire, Charlemagne's government was the most sophisticated Germanic administration until the thirteenth century. Charlemagne's kingdom spanned much of the western half of the old Roman Empire. Only Britain and Spain lay outside his jurisdiction. His association with the papacy allowed Charlemagne to portray himself as the protector of all Christians under the pope's obedience. As recognition of these facts, the bishop of Rome crowned Charlemagne emperor on Christmas Day, 800. The imperial coronation at the hands of the pope cemented the relationship between the empire and the Church.

D.   Carolingian Art

Before the Carolingians, Germanic art was largely abstract and decorative. Charlemagne wished to reestablish an artistic style more consonant with Roman culture. Artists from Italy and Byzantium came to the Carolingian court, but the Frankish artists created their own interpretations of the classical forms. More energized than ancient art, Carolingian presentations expressed the new culture resulting from the combination of Roman and Germanic societies.

V.   A Tour of Europe in the Ninth Century

A.   Introduction

The Carolingian kingdom provided the connective links between the Germanic and Slavic worlds of the north and the Islamic and Byzantine worlds of the Mediterranean. The medium of exchange in the commerce that flowed across Charlemagne's territories was the silver penny.

B.   England

At the outset of the ninth century, the king of Mercia was the strongest monarch of the Anglo-Saxon kingdoms. Mercia was surpassed by Wessex. Invasions of Scandinavian warriors, the Vikings, interrupted the expansion of Wessex. Bit by bit, the Vikings extended their control of England to include all but the kingdom of Wessex. King Alfred of Wessex not only forestalled a complete Viking victory, but began the process of uniting the various Anglo-Saxon kingdoms under the aegis of the king of Wessex. At his death, Alfred was only partly successful. The northeast of England remained in the hands of the Vikings.

C.   Scandinavia

Because of their expertise on the sea, the Scandinavians were the greatest long-distance traders of the early medieval West. Scandinavian society was little different from that of the Germanic tribes prior to their entry into the Roman Empire. A military aristocracy (*jarlar*) commanded a free society of farmers and herdsmen. Below the freemen were large numbers of slaves or thralls. By the eighth century the decentralized political organization of Scandinavia began to change in favor of three kings of Denmark, Norway, and Sweden. At about the same time as the creation of the kingdoms, extensive raiding began. The Swedes raided and settled along the shores of the Baltic and down the

Volga, Dvina, and Dneper Rivers as far as the Byzantine Empire. The Norwegians sailed westward to Ireland and the coast of the Frankish kingdom. The Danes were responsible for the settlement of England and Normandy in the kingdom of the Franks.

D.   The Slavic World

The Slavic world felt the political and commercial influences of the Scandinavian, Germanic, and Byzantine worlds. In the eighth century, the largest Slavic political confederation was the Moravian Empire, a prize sought both by the Byzantines and Carolingians. The Byzantine missionaries Cyril and Methodius enjoyed the first successes in Moravia; but in the mid-ninth century, the Carolingian king Louis the German conquered Moravia and imprisoned the Byzantine churchmen. The Magyars, an invader from the Asiatic steppes, in turn drove out the Franks and divided the Slavic world into northern and southern halves.

E.   Muslim Spain

The last of the Umayyad family, 'Abd ar-Rahman, established an independent emirate in Spain in 756. Like the emergence of the Carolingian empire, the coming of the Umayyads set off a cultural and economic renaissance.

VI.   After the Carolingians: From Empire to Lordships

For all its apparent successes, the Carolingian empire remained dependent on the uneasy partnership with the Frankish and Gallo-Roman aristocracy. As long as the empire expanded, there was plenty of land and booty with which to reward loyal followers. When in the course of the ninth century the empire was put on the defensive, rewards for the aristocracy were taken from the property of the kings. The return to the practice of dividing the kingdom among all the sons of the king weakened monarchical authority. In 843 the grandsons of Charlemagne separated the empire into three parts. The newly divided kingdoms were unable to meet the challenge of Scandinavian, Muslim, and Magyar attacks. The kings were equally unable to control the growth of regional authority in the hands of the aristocracy, who began to transform the offices of count and bishop into hereditary positions. Eventually new royal families arose from the regional aristocracy in preference to the ineffectual Carolingians. By the tenth century, the Germanic kingdom was no longer the model of political organization in western Europe.

TIMELINE

Insert the following events into the timeline. This should help you to compare important historical events chronologically.

Synod of Whitby   death of Theodoric the Ostrogoth
Charlemagne crowned emperor   death of Clovis
division of Carolingian empire into thirds   anointment of Pippin as king of Franks

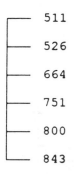

511

526

664

751

800

843

TERMS, PEOPLE, EVENTS

The following terms, people, and events are important to your understanding of the chapter. Define each one.

Theodoric the Ostrogoth   Gregory the Great   Lombards
Clovis   Anglo-Saxons   Columba
Augustine   Synod of Whitby   Franks
Cluny   counts   *ealdorman*
Charles Martel   Charlemagne   Carolingian Renaissance
missi dominici   capitularies   Utrecht Psalter
Offa of Mercia   Alfred of Wessex   *jarlar*
Harold Finehair   Moravia   Magyars
'Abd ar-Rahman I   al-Andalus

MAP EXERCISE

The following exercise is intended to clarify the geophysical environment and the spatial relationships among the important objects and places mentioned in the chapter. Locate the following places on the map.

Visigothic kingdom   Ostrogothic kingdom   Clovis' Frankish kingdom
Charlemagne's empire   Aachen   Anglo-Saxon kingdoms

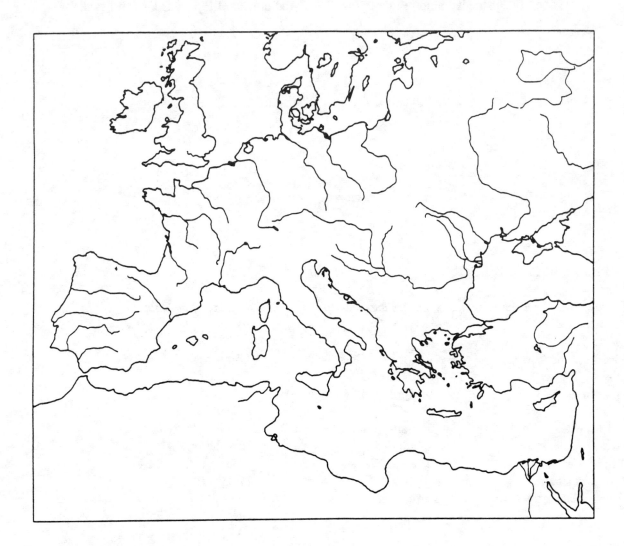

1. The geographical center of the Roman Empire was based on the Mediterranean. Where was the geographical center of the Carolingian Empire? How does this reflect a basic change in the orientation of Western Europe?

MAKING CONNECTIONS

The following questions are intended to emphasize important ideas within the chapter.

1. How successful were the Gothic kingdoms of Italy and northern Spain? What accounts for their demise? Why were the Franks and the Anglo-Saxons able to survive? How were they different from the Goths?

2. What three changes served to create a relatively homogeneous European peasantry? How did the combination of Gallo-Roman and Germanic traditions mold a homogeneous European aristocracy?

3. What were the limitations on early kingship?

4. How did Charlemagne construct an empire? How centralized was the government? Why did the empire disintegrate after his death?

5. What was the nature of the Carolingian Renaissance?

6. What political units surrounded the periphery of the Carolingian empire? How centralized were these kingdoms and caliphates?

PUTTING LARGER CONCEPTS TOGETHER

The following questions test your ability to summarize the major conclusions of the chapter.

1. How would you characterize the political organization of western Europe in the early Middle Ages? Did the creation of the Carolingian empire actually restore the centralized political structure of the ancient Roman Empire?

2. How significant was the Germanic stage of Western civilization? Defend your answer. Consider both social and political developments.

SELF-TEST OF FACTUAL INFORMATION

1. What factor tended to divide the Visigoths and their Lombard successors from the indigenous Gallo-Roman population?

    a. The Goths and Lombards were initially Arians and regarded as heretics by the indigenous population.
    b. The Goths were pagans.
    c. The Goths never established any formal kingships to govern the indigenous population.
    d. The Goths totally eradicated the Roman administration.

2. The Saxons, Angles, Jutes, Frisians, and Suebians who came to Britain

    a. enslaved or drove the natives into Wales and carved out their own small kingdoms.
    b. quickly coalesced their tribes into a unified kingdom.
    c. joined the Gallo-Frankish alliance against Justinian.
    d. rapidly left the island and returned to Germany.

3. Although Clovis ruled the Franks as king,

    a. he worked closely with the existing Gallo-Roman aristocracy to consolidate his power.
    b. real power rested in the Frankish tribal council.
    c. he was nothing more than a Roman general.
    d. the real authority was the Byzantine emperor.

4. Which of the following fundamental changes did *not* contribute to the transformation of rural society during the early Middle Ages?

    a. the virtual disappearance of Roman slavery
    b. the emergence of the household as the primary unit of social organization
    c. the spread of Christianity throughout the rural world
    d. the rapid formation of free and independent citizen-farmers

5. Which of the following statements concerning aristocratic women in the early Middle Ages is most accurate?

    a. Women played a smaller and less active role than in either Roman society or barbarian cultures.
    b. The religious life was closed to women.
    c. Women were permitted to inherit and dispose of property.
    d. Women were regarded as the equals of males.

6. The ecclesiastical policy that proved most crucial to Carolingian fortunes was

    a. the retention of Arianism.
    b. the alliance with the Roman papacy.
    c. the formation of the Dominicans.
    d. the strict separation of Church and state.

7. Cyril and Methodius

    a. rallied the Slavic peoples to resist Muslim subjugation.
    b. were instrumental in extending Roman cultural traditions into the Slavic world.
    c. developed a standard form of Slavic dress, style, and morality.
    d. laid the basis for a Slavic church and began a tradition of Slavic literacy.

8. What weakened the central authority of the Frankish empire after Charlemagne's death?

    a. competition among the descendants and grants to the aristocracy
    b. a series of peasant revolts and the decline in literacy
    c. an Anglo-Saxon invasion
    d. papal interference

9. What Saxon ruler was crowned emperor in 962?

    a. Henry the Fowler
    b. Conrad of Franconia
    c. Frederick Hohenstaufen
    d. Otto the Great

10. What monastery in eastern France was responsible for initiating Church reform in 909?

    a. St. Denis
    b. Cluny
    c. Citeaux
    d. Nivelles

Chapter 9

The High Middle Ages

OUTLINE

I.   The Royal Tombs at Fontevrault

The royal tombs in the monastic church at Fontevrault bind together eternally Eleanor of Aquitaine, her husband Henry II of England, and their son Richard the Lion-Hearted. While they rest together peacefully in death, their lives together were anything but pacific. Married to and divorced from King Louis VII of France, Eleanor's second marriage to Henry, the young Duke of Normandy, united the powerful inheritances of Normandy and Aquitaine. When Henry succeeded to the throne of England in 1154, the Angevin Empire was created. Henry refused to share the realities of royal authority with his wife and attempted to extend his power over Eleanor's provinces in southern France. Using her sons against their father, Eleanor attempted to regain her freedom of action. After several revolts, Henry locked his wife away for fourteen years. When Henry II died in 1189, he was succeeded by his son, Richard the Lion-Hearted. Much of Richard's ten-year reign was spent in campaigns in France or the Holy Land. In his absence, Eleanor ruled. When Richard in turn preceded his mother in death, Eleanor worked to secure the succession of her youngest surviving son, John. She finally died in 1202. Her life spanned the end of the era dominated by great feudal lords and the beginning of the period characterized by the growth of more centralized states.

II.   The Countryside

A.   Introduction

The economic and social transformation of Europe was just as dynamic as the political reform of the West. Increased population, economic productivity, and literacy reshaped European culture.

B.   The Peasantry: Serfs and Freemen

By the tenth century the medieval peasantry had become an undifferentiated class of dependent agricultural laborers. Their subservient status was reflected in lack of access to public courts, owed labor services, and payments in kind. Living conditions for the peasantry were generally poor. Between the eleventh and thirteenth centuries the amount of land under cultivation increased. Expansion at first created a demand for labor and allowed peasants to negotiate less onerous contracts with the landholding aristocracy. Eventually, customary service gave way to money payment and rents. In the western portions of Europe, the peasantry tended to become increasingly free of aristocratic control. As a result, the agricultural marketplace evolved into a commercial venture responding to the pressures of supply and demand. In the open market, some peasants flourished while others sank into landless poverty. In contrast to the western regions of Europe, the aristocratic landlords gained greater control over the peasantry of eastern Europe.

C.   The Aristocracy: Fighters and Breeders

The basis for aristocratic society was warfare. By definition, an aristocrat was a warrior, or knight. The classic example of feudal society existed in northern France. In some cases, this warrior elite descended from members of the noble clans of the Carolingian period. In order to limit membership in the aristocratic elite, inheritance was limited to a single heir—usually the oldest son. Daughters and younger sons were excluded from sharing in the distribution of wealth and land. By the twelfth century, the most important aristocratic families were virtually independent lords of the territories they controlled. Training for martial life began in youth and continued through the age of sixteen to eighteen, at which time young men were admitted formally into the ranks of knights. After knighthood, younger sons without access to land lived a bachelor lifestyle predicated on winning an estate or attracting attention through participation in military campaigns or mock warfare, the tournaments. Only those with access to land could marry and initiate a "house." Lifestyles for women were scarcely less dangerous. Women were eligible for marriage at age sixteen. They were primarily valued as childbearers. Numerous births reduced life expectancy for medieval women. As lineage was determined by male lines and as society was predicated on warfare, women lost social status. Aristocratic society was structured on the control of land and of agricultural workers or serfs who provided the labor. To obtain land, knights became vassals of greater lords. A vassal received land, or a fief, in return for loyalty and military service. Pyramids of vassalage and lordship created political hierarchies all over Europe. In England and the Latin kingdom of Jerusalem, the hierarchy of vassalage culminated in a single authority, the king. In other regions feudal loyalties were more local, and conflicting islands of lordship were created under counts and dukes.

D.   The Church: Saints and Monks

The Church sought to meet the needs of both the aristocratic warriors and the rural peasantry. Priests held mystical powers utilized to harness the supernatural on behalf of their parishioners. Saints were regarded as powerful intercessors between this world and eternity—often through the cult of the saints. Tombs were focal points for the cult of the saints. Many of these tombs were located in monasteries, and the monks directed the development of the cults. Monks also undertook the task of prayer for the souls of all departed Christians, not only the saints. Aristocrats made grants of land for the foundation of monasteries to ensure perpetual prayers for their souls after death. The Benedictines established the model for monastic lifestyle in western Europe. Benedictine life was predicated on obedience symbolized by the monks' submission to an ordered round of daily prayers. As the recipients of aristocratic largesse, monasteries rapidly accumulated large quantities of land and other types of wealth. Some within the monastic communities began to call for a return to simplicity and a separation from the material world. The Cistercians, under the leadership of Bernard of Clairvaux, tried to withdraw from the rest of the Christian community by establishing new monastic houses in the wildernesses of western Europe. The Church, through the Peace of God, attempted to curtail random violence typical of a society based on militarism.

E.   Crusaders: Soldiers of God

To redirect the martial vigor of aristocratic society, Pope Urban II called on Western knights to serve in an army dedicated to Christianity. The First Crusade resulted in the creation of feudal principalities in the Holy Land. As the first experiment in European overseas colonization, the feudal kingdoms of the crusaders made few accommodations with the religious and social customs of the Levant. Later crusades lost both the original pious fervor and the military success of the first. The Second Crusade, launched to prop up the crusader states, ended in military failure in Asia Minor. When Jerusalem fell to the Muslims, the Third Crusade attempted to recapture the holy city, but failed. The Fourth Crusade was sidetracked into an assault on the Byzantine capital of Constantinople. Subsequent Crusades won no military laurels. Crusades appealed to younger sons of the feudal nobility and lesser knights, who saw in them opportunities to obtain land and enhance their social status. Although often glorified, Crusades were less than noble military exercises in greed more than piety. The crusading ethic often included anti-Semitism and indiscriminant slaughter of innocents. When kings of more centralized states came to see the Crusades as wasteful, the era of the Crusade came to an end.

III.   Medieval Towns

A.   Introduction

Towns represented the social opposite of the rural countryside. Serfdom did not exist there, nor did most towns recognize the authority of the military aristocracy. Towns were, however, the purveyors of manufactured goods and services sought by all members of rural society.

B.   Italian Communes

In the Italian peninsula, unlike elsewhere in western Europe, urbanism had never disappeared during the Germanic invasions. By the eleventh century, Italian towns asserted their supremacy as commercial centers, carrying trade throughout the Mediterranean. Urban fleets both carried goods and protected traders. Greater cities, such as Venice and Genoa, established colonies of merchants at the ends of trade routes to China and the East. The Crusades offered opportunities for extending the commercial empires of the Italian towns. In 1204 crusaders under the direction of the Venetians actually captured Constantinople, the capital of the Byzantine Empire. International trade spurred the development of merchant law, business administration, bookkeeping, and credit contracts. Despite the antipathy of the Church, credit became the foundation for the expansion of medieval commerce. By the twelfth century, Italian towns sought to declare their independence from regional lords and expressed their solidarity by the creation of urban communes. Communes established their own jurisdictions over prices, markets, and taxation. The communes were divided in loyalties between magnates who controlled the communal government and the popular corporations who controlled the guild organization of commerce and crafts. Disputes between magnates and populars often erupted into open conflict and alliance with outside forces, the German empire or the papacy. Italian urban government consisted of a series of councils. All males were members of the *arengo* or assembly. As the *arengo* was normally too unwieldy to carry on the actual functions of government, smaller working councils carried on the actual tasks of administration. Executive authority of the communes resided with consuls. In order to overcome the tendency to factionalism within the commune, trained public administrators, the *podestas,* were often hired.

C.   Northern Towns

Commercial activity in northern Europe centered around the northern seas, the Baltic and the North. The greatest concentration of urbanism in northern Europe was located in the Low Countries at the mouth of the Rhine River. Town growth was based on the development of the woolen cloth industry. The social organization of northern towns differed from that of Italy due to the absence of an aristocratic group of magnates. At the top of the society of northern European towns were the wholesale merchants or patricians who purchased raw materials and sold the finished products. The wholesale merchants monopolized urban government. Next were the masters of the craft guilds who controlled the production of woolen cloth through the processes of weaving, dyeing, and fulling. At the bottom were the unskilled and semiskilled laborers in the employ of the guild masters. Providing a conduit for the exchange of goods between the northern towns and the Italian towns were the fairs of Champagne, annual markets located in the very center of Europe in eastern France. Products from north and south, both luxuries and more mundane items, were bought and sold in these fairs.

D.   Urban Culture

Towns spawned a religious culture and lifestyle peculiarly urban. Universities developed out of the early cathedral schools where the educational emphasis was on the ancient tradition of the trivium and quadrivium. With the expansion of urban life, education separated from the control of the bishops and the cathedral clergy. At Bologna in Italy, the study of law and the preparation of professional urban administrators were the focal point of the educational system. Students, who were customarily not citizens of the town, formed their own guild or *universitas* that controlled the curriculum, the appointment of instructors, and the conditions of life.

In northern Europe, Paris emerged as the greatest educational center. Unlike Bologna, the guilds of the university at Paris were composed of masters. Student life at the university was often rough and rowdy. At the outset of the thirteenth century, the study of Aristotle consumed the theologians of the University of Paris. Received through the intermediation of Muslim philosophers in Spain, Aristotle became the chief authority for scholasticism. At first, the authorities of the Church regarded the application of Aristotelian logic as heretical. It was Thomas Aquinas who bridged the chasm between Aristotle and ecclesiastical orthodoxy. Aquinas applied Aristotelian philosophy to the most important theological questions.

Monasticism with its demands for isolation was not well suited to the urban lifestyle. In the environment of the town, the orders of friars fulfilled the need for a militant Christian vocation. Dedicated to the controversial principle of poverty, Francis of Assisi founded the Friars Minor or Franciscans. The Franciscans devoted themselves to public preaching and to education. Similarly, the Dominicans, named for their founder, were dedicated to Christian evangelism and teaching. Both orders became mainstays of the universities of Europe.

IV.   TheInvention of the State

A.   Introduction

Two types of political entities existed in the Middle Ages. The papacy and the Germanic Empire laid claim to universal authority. The kingdoms of France and England were more limited in their concept of government.

B.   The Universal States: Empire and Papacy

Although the Carolingian empire had lapsed, the Germanic traditions were less disturbed in the easternmost territories. There the empire was restored under the Saxon dukes of northern Germany, particularly Otto I (936-973). In order to establish some sort of administration, the Saxons relied heavily on the bishops and archbishops of Germany and Italy. The emperors, whose office remained elective, were never able to subdue fully the other members of the German aristocracy. In addition to the clergy, emperors appointed technically unfree servants called ministerials to defend strategic points within the empire. By the twelfth century, the ministerials achieved freedom and added to the welter of conflicting jurisdictions in Germany as imperial knights. From Otto I on, German emperors were intent on control of northern Italy and the papacy. In the long run, Germany was abandoned to facilitate the Italian policies of successive dynasties. In particular, the imperial involvement with the papacy was a fatal entanglement. Emperor Henry III initiated a period of papal reform. From this secular beginning, clerical reformers tried to free the Church from imperial control. At the heart of the struggle for independence was the issue of "lay investiture." The issue reached a crisis during the reign of Pope Gregory VII (1073–1084) and resulted in armed conflict between the supporters of the papacy and the emperor. The debate was not settled until the Concordat of Worms in 1122. Papal authority after the middle of the twelfth century was based increasingly on the development of an ecclesiastical legal system, the canon law. Church courts were established in every diocese in western Europe. Moreover, the canon law empowered the popes to make new laws at will. The use of the canon law reached its height under Pope Innocent III (1198–1216). During his reign, the Fourth Lateran Council was called to define the fundamental doctrines of the Church. Despite papal successes, the ability of the papacy to enforce its will throughout western Europe was called into question at the end of the thirteenth century. Monarchs of centralized secular states such as England and France successfully opposed the papacy, sometimes with force.

C.   The Nation-States: France and England

Kings, unlike emperors, claimed only regional rather than universal authority. The kings of France began as regional aristocrats surrounded by peers who were in many cases more powerful than the kings. France was favored by a dynasty, the Capetians, who continuously provided male heirs from 987 to 1314. From their capital at Paris, the Capetians slowly built a more centralized kingdom. The founder of a united France was King Philip II Augustus (1180–1223) who acquired enormous territories by marriage alliances, warfare, and crusade. He established a new administrative system based on salaried agents called *baillis*, who administered justice and collected royal taxes. A permanent central court system staffed with professional jurists was the creation of Philip's grandson, Louis IX. Gradually the power and independence of the regional aristocrats in France declined.

The centralized kingdom of England was the creation of the Norman Conquest of 1066. William the Conqueror retained portions of the administrative system of Anglo-Saxon England while imposing the French system of feudal vassalage. All land in England was held directly from the king. William's successors created a central treasury system, the Exchequer and a central court. The most important legal reformer was Henry II (1154–1189). Henry successfully imposed the jurisdiction of royal courts over both aristocratic and ecclesiastical tribunals. Under King John (1199–1216) and Henry III (1216–1272), the barons of England were able to gain some voice in the government. John was forced to accept the Magna Carta, or great charter of liberties that placed the English king under the rule of law. King Edward I (1272–1307) formalized the participation of barons in government by the creation of a parliament. As the wealth of the towns made them attractive sources of revenue, urban representatives also became customary attenders at parliament. By 1300 England and France had become the most centralized governments of western Europe. Because their governments could make more efficient use of their national resources, they were also the most powerful.

TIMELINE

Insert the following events into the timeline. This should help you to compare important historical events chronologically.

signing of Magna Carta in England   election of Hugh Capet as king of France
charter granted to University of Paris   beginning of reign of Philip II Augustus
Urban II calls First Crusade   meeting of Henry IV and Gregory VII at Canossa

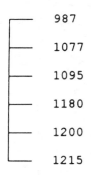

987

1077

1095

1180

1200

1215

TERMS, PEOPLE, EVENTS

The following terms, people, and events are important to your understanding of the chapter. Define each one.

demesne	knight	vassal
fief	saints	*lectio divina*
feudalism	Truce of God	Crusades
arengo	*podesta*	communes
patricians	*Decretum Gratiani*	University of Bologna
University of Paris	Thomas Aquinas	Dominicans
Franciscans	Otto I the Great	Saxon dynasty
Salian dynasty	Staufen dynasty	ministerials
lay investiture	Concordat of Worms	Frederick I Barbarossa
Innocent III	Magna Carta	parliament
Fourth Lateran Council	Capetian dynasty	Philip II Augustus
baillis	*seneschals*	Louis IX
William the Conqueror	sheriffs	Henry II of England

MAP EXERCISE

The following exercise is intended to clarify the geophysical environment and the spatial relationships among the important objects and places mentioned in the chapter. Locate the following places on the map.

northern boundary of the ancient Roman Empire around A.D. 180
boundaries of the following states: Holy Roman Empire, France, England

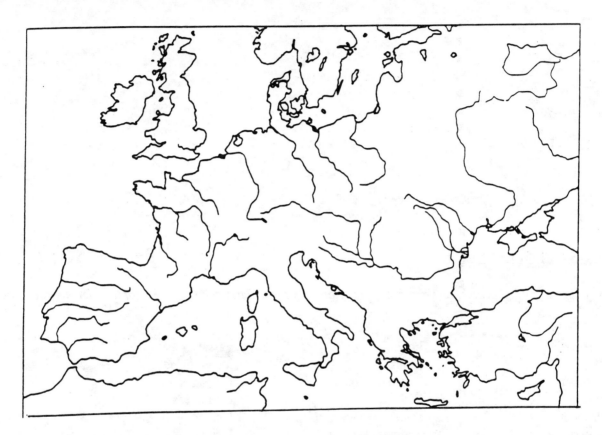

1.   How did the political boundaries of the medieval states compare with those of the ancient Roman Empire? In what direction did the expansion take place?

2.   How many political units were there in the medieval world? How did this compare to the ancient West? How did it compare to the period of the Carolingian Empire?

MAKING CONNECTIONS

The following questions are intended to emphasize important ideas within the chapter.

1. How did the peasantry change after the tenth century? What were the differences between the peasantries of eastern and western Europe?

2. What was feudalism? What was the function of men and women within feudalism? What was the function of the Church in feudal society?

3. What was the political and social organization of Italian towns? How did the political and social organization of northern towns differ?

4. What was a university? What was the nature of university education? Why was Aristotle of such importance?

5. How centralized was the German empire? Why did the claims of the emperor naturally conflict with the claims of the pope?

6. What were the steps in the creation of a centralized monarchy in France? What were the stages in the creation of a centralized monarchy in England? What element was present in England but not France?

PUTTING LARGER CONCEPTS TOGETHER

The following questions test your ability to summarize the major conclusions of the chapter.

1. Why did Europe fail to restore the unity of the ancient empire? What aspects of European society dictated particularism rather than centralization? In what sense did feudalism contribute to particularism?

2. Which states of Europe were more successful in achieving centralization? Why? Where do the cities fit into the pattern of centralization and particularism?

SELF-TEST OF FACTUAL INFORMATION

1. Among the military aristocracy, the rule of inheritance usually provided that

   a. all children should divide the estate equally.
   b. only male children should divide the estate equally.
   c. only the oldest male child should inherit.
   d. the strongest and most capable male heir should inherit.

2. What best describes the Church's attitude toward women?

   a. The Church revered them as models of Christian piety.
   b. The Church saw them as descendants of the Virgin Mary.
   c. The Church portrayed them as the source of evil and corruption.
   d. The Church urged that they be admitted to the priesthood.

3. The most important of the supernatural powers harnessed by the Church was

   a. the saints.
   b. magic.
   c. absolution of sin.
   d. prayer.

4. Which of the following statements concerning the Crusades is most accurate?

   a. The Crusades continually carved out greater portions of the Middle East, until most of the land as far as Persia was under the control of Western knights.
   b. Crusaders rapidly adopted social and religious customs similar to those of the indigenous inhabitants of the Crusader states.
   c. Crusaders were most often younger sons or landless knights seeking opportunities to increase their social status through land.
   d. The concept of crusade was limited to war carried out in the name of Christianity against the Muslims.

5. Which of the following institutions was *not* found in the political culture of Italian towns?

   a. *podestas*
   b. societies of knights
   c. communes
   d. monarchy

6. Where were the great fairs that facilitated trade between northern and southern Europe located?

   a. Burgundy
   b. England
   c. Champagne
   d. Venice

7. The *Decretum Gratiani* prepared at Bologna in 1140 was a significant treatise on

    a. cuisine.
    b. political science.
    c. Church law.
    d. mathematics.

8. Who is credited with founding the scholastic method?

    a. Peter Abelard
    b. Peter Lombard
    c. Thomas Aquinas
    d. Averroes

9. The Germanic empire could best be described as

    a. restricted strictly to northern Germany.
    b. decentralized with many competing jurisdictions.
    c. highly centralized with an efficient central administration.
    d. in total control of the papacy.

10. The creator of French territorial integrity was

    a. Philip II Augustus.
    b. Hugh Capet.
    c. Frederick II.
    d. Innocent III.

Chapter 10

The Later Middle Ages, 1300–1500

OUTLINE

I.   Webs of Stone and Blood

By the end of the fourteenth century, the centralized states of western Europe were disturbed by war, dynastic confusion, and economic depression. Great aristocratic families made use of the collapse of the centralized states to create new political and economic allegiances. Similarly, new architectural forms, such as that of the cathedral of Saint Vitus in Prague, broke with French Gothic, the previously dominant style.

II.   Politics as a Family Affair

A.   Introduction

Fragmented and regionally diffuse landholdings typified the aristocratic families of the fourteenth and fifteenth centuries. Aristocratic power threatened the centralized political authorities of the later Middle Ages.

B.   The Struggle for Central Europe

Five aristocratic families struggled for control of the Germanic empire—the houses of Luxembourg, Wittelsbach, Habsburg, Premysl, and Anjou. Each family shifted its seat of power from western Europe to the eastern frontiers of the Germanic empire. Joining the great families in the subjection of eastern Europe were the Teutonic Knights, a crusading order that transferred its activities to the Slavic regions along the Baltic Sea. The economy of the new eastern Europe was varied. Peasants were transported from Germany into the formerly Slavic regions to support the development of an agricultural system dedicated to the commercial export of grain. In the southern regions of the frontier, discoveries of metals led to the creation of a flourishing mining industry. Dynasties established in the eastern kingdoms of Bohemia, Hungary, Poland, and the duchy of Austria existed as a result of alliances with the regional aristocracy. Typical of the eastern dynasts was Charles IV, king of Bohemia and emperor. Charles assiduously added to his power base as king of Bohemia, but decreed his disinterest in centralizing his authority as emperor. In the Golden Bull of 1356, Charles recognized the autonomy of the major princes and kings within the Germanic empire. While major states continued to develop on the eastern frontier of the empire, the western portions fragmented into literally thousands of tiny jurisdictions under bishops, imperial towns, and imperial knights. The Holy Roman Empire was not united as a state until the nineteenth century.

C.   A Hundred Years of War

Competing aristocratic families also disturbed the political equanimity of western Europe. In Spain, the process of recovering the peninsula for Christianity left three squabbling kingdoms. Unity was only achieved after the marriage of Ferdinand of Aragon and Isabella of Castile in 1469. In northern Europe, the centralized monarchies of France and England engaged in the Hundred Years' War. Causes of the conflict were the English king's status as vassal of the French king for his territories in Gascony, English support for the urban rebellions in Flanders against the king of France, and the English king's claim to the throne of France after the end of the Capetian dynasty in 1314. While dynastic disputes were the stated reason for the onset of war, the code of chivalry required the elites of England and France to engage in violent conduct. The greater size and wealth of France gave that nation a competitive advantage in warfare, but England's greater administrative efficiency offset the natural French advantages. Armies were no longer feudal levies, but paid mercenaries and military specialists. The English army had more recent experience in newer forms of warfare and was better commanded. Not surprisingly, English armies, even when outnumbered, won the major engagements of the war. Raiding and pillaging between campaigns also destroyed much of the French countryside. Because the French kings could neither defeat the English armies nor protect the countryside from pillage, aristocratic families began to carve out independent principalities. The most important withdrawal was the duchy of Burgundy, which actually allied itself with England against the French king. Just as it appeared a total English victory might occur, a mystical peasant girl, Joan of Arc, galvanized the French army to victory before her capture and execution in 1431. Exhausted by the years of warfare, the English were pressed back to the coasts of France. The conflict ended in 1453 with the English in command of the solitary French port of Calais. As in France, continuous warfare benefited the growing power and autonomy of the aristocracy in England. Increasing aristocratic factionalism resulted in civil war from 1455 to 1485. The Wars of the Roses, the dynastic struggle between cadet branches of the English royal family and their allies, culminated in the arrival of a new royal family. The Tudor dynasty came to the throne of England in 1485.

III.   Life and Death in the Later Middle Ages

A.   Introduction

The military violence typical of the later Middle Ages was mirrored in the social upheaval of the times. Population growth had stretched the agricultural system beyond its ability to produce. Shortly after 1300, famine and plague struck the European population. The greatest disaster to ever strike Europe, the effects of the Black Death were felt more strongly in western Europe.

B.   Dancing With Death

Shortly after the beginning of the fourteenth century, the supply of food failed to meet the needs of the European population. Famine was followed by epidemic disease. In 1347 the plague reached Europe from central Asia. In five years the plague killed between one-half and one-third of the population. Medical knowledge was rudimentary; and people attributed the onset of the disease to divine wrath, Jewish plots, or astrological conjunctions. Nothing, of course, halted the progress of the epidemic. After the first five-year outbreak of the plague, the disease revisited Europe continually until the eighteenth century. The Black Death imposed many changes on European society. Psychologically, the artistic outlook turned toward a fascination with the imagery of death. The European economy drifted into depression. The traditional social structures that had bound lord and laborer were shattered.

C.   The Plague of Insurrection

The plague dramatically reduced the supply of labor and, thus, increased its market value. Peasants anticipated more favorable contractual terms for land and labor. Lords responded by demanding legislation to fix prices and wages. Similarly, craft masters attempted to gain greater restrictions on the wages of urban laborers. When in addition kings seeking new sources of revenue for warfare increased taxation, the result was revolution in both towns and countryside. In France the peasants' revolt against the authority of both the aristocracy and the Church was called the Jacquerie. At the same time, Parisian merchants also demanded reforms of the royal government. After a brief time, the military aristocracy made short work of both the peasant revolutionaries and the Parisian merchants. Similar peasant rebellions broke out in England in 1381, in Spain in 1395, and in Germany throughout the fourteenth and fifteenth centuries. Urban revolts of guildsmen and laborers were also commonplace. Popular revolts became a permanent feature of European political relationships.

D.   Living and Dying in Medieval Towns

The Black Death drastically affected the urban economy of the medieval West. Demand for Italian manufactured goods and commercial activity fell. As English and French kings under wartime pressure repeatedly reneged on loans, the great banking houses of Italy experienced bankruptcy. As Italians lost their commercial dominance, German towns moved to fill the void. The Hanseatic League, a coalition of northern German towns, cooperated in the establishment of markets throughout Europe. English towns based on a native woolen cloth industry also revived as the Flemish towns waned. Conditions after the plague widened the gap between urban poor and wealthy merchants. Fear of potential revolution created two seemingly contradictory responses: development of public assistance and repression. Towns began to take over hospitals and poorhouses formerly run by charitable and ecclesiastical organizations. Some towns created centralized relief services charged with all public assistance. At the same time, limits were placed on begging and legal punishments became more draconian. Public executions for all sorts of offenses became commonplace.

IV.   The Spirit of the Later Middle Ages

A.   Introduction

Political disarray was reflected in divisions within the Church during the later Middle Ages.

B.   Christendom Divided

The first crisis within the Church was the so-called Babylonian captivity. In 1305 Clement V, a Frenchmen, established the papal court at Avignon rather than in Rome. Although in the Germanic empire, Avignon placed the pope under the tutelage of the king of France. For seventy years, Frenchmen dominated the Church. While the political influence of the papacy declined, the popes at Avignon distinguished themselves by the creation of an enormously efficient system of ecclesiastical taxation. One of the most important sources of income was the sale of indulgences, payment of money to assist departed souls in their penance. The other important source of revenue was the sale of Church offices. The second crisis of the Church was the Schism, created when more than one pope held office at the same time. In 1377 Pope Gregory XI returned to Rome, but died immediately. The Roman mobs demanded the election of an Italian pope and threatened violence. Cowed by the overt threat, the cardinals present in Rome chose Urban VI, an Italian bishop. A second election was then held that resulted in the election of a French candidate, Clement VII. The Schism divided the obedience of the Church into two warring camps. France and Scotland recognized Clement in Avignon. Germany and England chose Urban in Rome. University of Paris scholars and Church lawyers suggested that only a general council of all Christendom could end the dispute. The first attempt, the Council of Pisa of 1408, was unsuccessful. Neither pope recognized the council's authority, and the result was the addition of a third pope to the Schism. A second council, the Council of Constance, finally resolved the split. The period of the Schism (1377-1415) badly damaged the prestige and universal authority of the papacy.

C.   Discerning the Spirit of God

The decline of the institutional Church gave greater emphasis to less orthodox religious views. Witchcraft was not a social fixation of the Middle Ages, but became a major concern of ecclesiastical authorities after the fifteenth century. As respect for the established Church diminished, Christians sought more direct relationships with the divine through mysticism and charismatic societies. Male groups tended to focus on the doctrine of apostolic poverty still emphasized by the radical branch of the Franciscans. Female mystics concentrated on Eucharistic theology and on mystical visions of spiritual union with God. Mysticism always bordered on heresy, particularly in the eyes of the established Church. John Wycliffe and Jan Hus were the most prominent heretics of the later Middle Ages. Wycliffe was an Englishman who attacked the wealth and property of the Church—a view supported by the English crown—as well as the authority of priests, the efficacy of indulgences, and the sanctity of the clergy. His teachings were carried to the kingdom of Bohemia where priests at the University of Prague picked them up. The leader of the Bohemian movement was Jan Hus. Adopted by the Czech nationalist movement, Hus became not only a voice for religious reform but also a rallying point against the German elite. At the Council of Constance, Hus was convicted of heresy, condemned, and burned at the stake. His death set off a Czech rebellion in Bohemia. Although the revolt fragmented and finally failed, Bohemia remained a Hussite stronghold until the sixteenth century Protestant Reformation.

D.   William of Ockham and the Spirit of Truth

In the later Middle Ages, the union of philosophy and theology was split asunder. The creator of the new age of philosophical doubt was William of Ockham, an English Franciscan. William was a member of the radical branch of the Franciscans, who became a pamphleteer for the emperor in opposition to the authority of the popes. Philosophically, Ockham argued that no general conclusions concerning theology could be demonstrated by rational argument. His school of thought was called radical nominalism—he believed that general conclusions, or universals, could not be deduced from specific cases. Therefore, nothing could be known as a result of philosophical or theological speculation. Ockham's radical nominalism dominated the universities after his death during the Black Death. Students began to pay greater attention to investigation of specific observations rather than engage in philosophical generalizations.

E.   Vernacular Literature and the Individual

As regionalism became more pronounced in the later Middle Ages, varieties of vernacular literature rivaled the dominance of Latin prose and poetry. Most notable among the vernacular authors were the Italians, Dante Alighieri, Petrarch, and Boccaccio. Dante's *Divine Comedy*, an account of the author's heroic quest through hell, purgatory, and paradise, remains a timeless classic. The work was a personalized evaluation of medieval society in 1300. England also enjoyed a literary revitalization. William Langland and Geoffrey Chaucer, like Dante, used literary means to critique their contemporary societies. Chaucer's *Canterbury Tales* covered the gamut of English society from the very poor to the elite. In many ways French literature provided the models for vernacular works in all languages. Unique among later medieval authors was a French woman, Christine de Pisan, who supported herself and her family as a writer. She is virtually the sole voice presenting a feminist view of the Middle Ages.

TIMELINE

Insert the following events into the timeline. This should help you to compare important historical events chronologically.

beginning of Hundred Years' War	Council of Constance ends Great Schism
Black Death first strikes Europe	death of John Wycliffe
death of William of Ockham	beginning of Babylonian captivity at Avignon

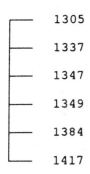

1305

1337

1347

1349

1384

1417

TERMS, PEOPLE, EVENTS

The following terms, people, and events are important to your understanding of the chapter. Define each one.

Joan of Arc	Wars of the Roses	Holy Roman Empire
Emperor Charles IV	Golden Bull	Black Death
Jacquerie	Etienne Marcel	Hanseatic League
Avignon	indulgences	benefices
Great Schism	conciliarist	Council of Constance
Witches' Hammer	John Wycliffe	Lollards
Jan Hus	William of Ockham	nominalism
Dante Alighieri	*The Divine Comedy*	Geoffrey Chaucer
The Canterbury Tales	Christine de Pisan	Hundred Years' War

MAP EXERCISE

The following exercise is intended to clarify the geophysical environment and the spatial relationships among the important objects and places mentioned in the chapter. Locate the following places on the map.

kingdom of France   kingdom of England   Holy Roman Empire
Avignon   Rome   Bohemia
Austria

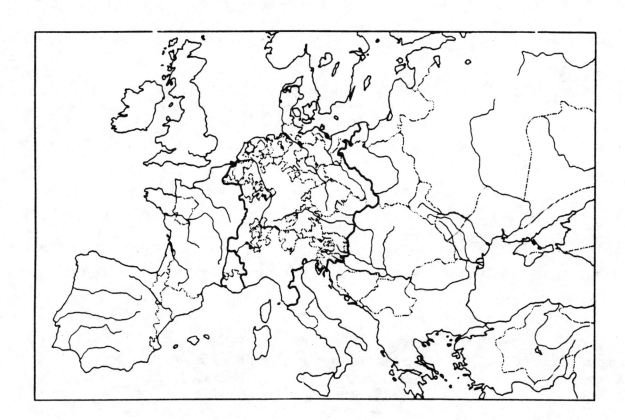

1. In what part of Europe were the most centralized governments located? In what part of Europe was there little or no centralization? What accounts for this political orientation? How is it related to the formation of feudal forms of government? Were the most centralized governments in formerly feudal kingdoms?

MAKING CONNECTIONS

The following questions are intended to emphasize important ideas within the chapter.

1. What were the causes of the Hundred Years' War? Who won? What was the impact on the two nations involved?

2. How did eastern Europe develop politically and economically? What was the impact of the Golden Bull on the Holy Roman Empire?

3. What was the Black Death? How did it affect Europe socially and politically?

4. What towns benefited from the decline of the urban centers of Italy?

5. How did the residence of the papacy at Avignon and the Great Schism affect the Church? What was conciliarism?

6. What was the nature of popular religious belief in the later Middle Ages? How did William of Ockham affect the development of medieval speculative theology?

7. How did the development of literature in the vernacular reflect political trends in Europe?

PUTTING LARGER CONCEPTS TOGETHER

The following questions test your ability to summarize the major conclusions of the chapter.

1. To many Europeans living in the post-1350 Middle Ages, the events they witnessed seemed to presage the end of the world. How did the events of the later Middle Ages reflect the four horsemen of the Apocalypse—famine, pestilence, war, and death. Were they right? Was Europe fundamentally different in political and social structure as a result of the catastrophes of the later Middle Ages?

2. Compare the fates of the two institutions that claimed universal authority in medieval Europe—the papacy and the Holy Roman Empire. What were the forces that destroyed the claims to universal authority in each case?

SELF-TEST OF FACTUAL INFORMATION

1. The Golden Bull issued by Charles IV in 1356

    a. abolished the office of emperor in the Holy Roman Empire.
    b. recognized the various German princes and kings as autonomous rulers.
    c. divided the Holy Roman Empire into three parts.
    d. granted the papacy the right to select the candidates for Holy Roman Emperor.

2. Which of the following conditions was not in France's favor at the outset of the Hundred Years' War?

    a. a larger and more densely populated kingdom
    b. three to five times greater wealth
    c. a king who was a better administrator and military commander
    d. a greater industrial base

3. For England, defeat in the Hundred Years' War caused

    a. increased restlessness that spawned sixteenth-century expansion.
    b. a fifteenth-century civil war between two competing families for the throne.
    c. growth in commercial enterprises that resulted in mercantilism.
    d. a decline in nationalism that, in turn, caused Scotland and Wales to seek independence.

4. Following the first outbreak of the plague,

    a. Europe was able to ward off subsequent aftershocks.
    b. medical science discovered its cause and a potent vaccine to fight the disease.
    c. it returned with milder repercussions.
    d. its aftershocks were even more catastrophic.

5. During the second half of the fourteenth century, the Hanseatic League

    a. brokered mercenary armies for the many European wars.
    b. explored the New World.
    c. monopolized most of the European bullion supply.
    d. monopolized the northern grain trade and the export of Scandinavian fish throughout Europe.

6. At the same time that towns began to organize public assistance, they also attempted to

    a. eliminate poverty through public works programs.
    b. drive prices higher to withdraw money from the poorer population.
    c. control more strictly the activities of the urban poor through repressive police and judicial procedures.
    d. restrict the charity of the Church.

7. Frustrated politically, the fourteenth-century popes at Avignon were successful in perfecting the Church's

   a. liturgy.
   b. reform of the laity.
   c. legal and fiscal systems.
   d. social and cultural traditions.

8. What council was responsible for ending the Great Schism?

   a. Pisa
   b. Trent
   c. Constance
   d. Nicaea

9. Which of the following statements best describes the political philosophy of William of Ockham?

   a. Papal authority is sanctified by God and not subject to human judgment.
   b. The canon law represents the highest court, thus the papacy's power is not subject to review in secular courts.
   c. There is a delicate balance between faith and reason; hence, a combination of the council of the cardinals and secular monarchs should elect the pope.
   d. Imperial power is derived from the people, not the pope; hence, government is entirely secular and neither popes, nor bishops, nor priests have any role.

10. All of the following were authors of major vernacular works in the later Middle Ages *except*

    a. Christine de Pisan.
    b. Geoffrey Chaucer.
    c. Dante Alighieri.
    d. Humbert of Silva Candida.

Chapter 11

The Italian Renaissance

OUTLINE

I.   A Civic Procession

Gentile Bellini's painting *The Procession of the Relic of the Holy Cross* recounts visually the miraculous healing of a young boy due to the intervention of the patron saint of Venice. More than the event, the city itself and its urban society are glorified in the work of art.

II.   Renaissance Society

A.   Introduction

The Renaissance was initiated in the midst of the devastation of the Black Death. Unlike the Middle Ages, the Renaissance placed particular value on the renewal of classical art forms and literature and on the importance of the individual. Associated with Italy more than any other region of Europe, the Renaissance initiated a period of dramatic change. The entire age can be subdivided into three phases: from 1350 to 1400 during which discovery of ancient texts and experimentation with new art forms took place, 1400 to 1500 typified by political stability in the Italian city-states and the creation of a recognizable culture, and 1500 to 1550 dominated by foreign invasion and the diffusion of the Italian Renaissance to the rest of western Europe.

B.   The Environment

Italy was distinguished from the rest of Europe by the degree of its urbanization. Not only were seven of the ten largest European towns located in the Italian peninsula, but the region also was dotted with numerous smaller towns as well. Surrounding each city was a rural area that served as a supplier of foodstuffs and as a region of recruitment for the urban population. The cities served as central markets for the produce of their agricultural hinterlands. In the aftermath of the plague, Italian cities were smaller than their modern counterparts. Despite the diminution of the population, urban space was crowded with men, markets, animals, and agricultural products. The social organization of towns differed from the countryside, where social status was determined by one's relationship to the land. In the city, social distinction was determined by occupation and membership in guilds, communal organizations that imposed monopolies of trade or production. At the top of the guild structure were wholesale merchants, bankers, and public administrators. Farther down the social scale were retail merchants and skilled craftsmen. At the bottom were those men, unskilled and underemployed laborers, who were not guild members. Urban society was typified by a huge gulf between rich and poor. In Florence, ten percent of the population held ninety percent of all wealth in the city. Such disparities were common in Renaissance cities.

C.   Production and Consumption

Demographics shaped the change in market forces in the early Renaissance. Between 1350 and 1400, the plague and subsequent aftershocks continued to depress the population of all areas. As a result, the value of labor increased. In the short run, the agricultural laborers' disposable wealth—that amount left after the purchase of necessities—went up. Simultaneously, investment in the traditional fashion, in land and in the cloth industry, brought diminished returns for wealthy capitalists in the cities. Both the poor and the rich, each group with greater amounts of disposable wealth, turned to the purchase of luxuries. Such purchases eased the psychological burden of the plague and aided in escaping the increasing burdens of taxation. Producers responded to the sudden demand for luxuries by expanding markets in silks, jewelry, imported foodstuffs, and art objects. In a sense, the culture of the Renaissance was the creation of the plague.

D.   The Experience of Life

Life in a Renaissance city could be hard, particularly for the poor. Children of the poor often failed to survive childhood. For those young who survived, males were apprenticed and females were sent out as domestic servants. Children of the wealthy were more likely to survive past their early years. There was no standard for Renaissance families. Most were probably nuclear in structure, but there were examples of several generations—grandparents, siblings, grandchildren, and servants—living under a single roof. Even nuclear households often contained servants. Older children were dealt with as economic resources and utilized to increase the economic fortunes of the household. Sons were normally apprenticed at age ten or thereafter. Daughters' fortunes were determined by the ability of the family to arrange for a dowry. Young women with dowries were married and entered the household of their husbands until such time as the new couple had sufficient wealth to establish a separate household. Those without dowries were hired out as domestic servants or entered convents. Women commonly were married at around age twenty to men ten or more years their seniors. Married life for women normally involved successive pregnancies. Only death and the age differential between men and women limited family size. Men married much later in life, after long supervision in the households of other males. Some males never were able to establish independent households. Delayed household formation may have led to sexual frustration and even homosexuality. Men who did successfully establish independent households enjoyed complete authority over those under their roofs. Death was a companion of the Renaissance household. Frequent outbreaks of the plague and lack of medical knowledge ensured annual harvests of those without natural defenses—often the very young and adolescents. Famine and starvation were less significant causes of death.

E.   The Quality of Life

Despite the plague, the quality of life for surviving citizens of the Renaissance may have improved. Life spans increased for survivors as a result of more plentiful food supplies and more varied diets. Social and political cohesion also increased as citizens came to depend on a greater variety of social support groups. Kinship groups were supplemented by guilds, neighborhood organizations—either familial or ecclesiastical—and godparenting. The Church remained central to Renaissance society. The fundamental symbols of daily ritual were derived from ecclesiastical sources. The calendar of the Church continued to establish the rhythms of urban life. Even spatial relationships within towns were dependent on the location of individual churches and parish boundaries. The extent to which Renaissance citizens were able to express social solidarity with the city in which they resided can be observed in the works of art produced within the shops and schools of Italy. In many cases, works of art were expressions of civic pride.

III.   Renaissance Art

A.   Introduction

The art of the Renaissance owed as much to the social system in which the artists lived and worked as to the individual genius and techniques of the artists. Wealth within the cities permitted the creation of public works of art—buildings and monumental sculpture. The celebration of the individual and the existence of disposable wealth led to a sudden interest in portraiture. Renaissance art was also the product of a system of education based on the principles of the craft guilds. Students worked as members of shops where wealthy patrons contracted specific works of art. It was, in short, a business. Most Renaissance artists became skilled in more than one area of expertise. The great geniuses of the Renaissance were equally renowned for their architectural, sculptural, and painted works.

B.   An Architect, a Sculptor, and a Painter

The early Renaissance produced three artistic masters who dominated their respective fields. Brunelleschi combined classical architectural motifs—in particular the dome and round windows —with concepts already present in late Gothic architecture to produce a radically new style. His greatest triumph was the dome atop the cathedral in Florence. In sculpture, Donatello was the most important early Renaissance innovator. Again, Donatello impressed classical concepts of the ideal form on the sculpture of the later Gothic period. Among his contributions was a renewed interest in the equestrian monumental statue, a common feature of public art in antiquity. Masaccio introduced the mathematical science of linear perspective to Renaissance painting. His innovation gave paintings the illusion of three-dimensional space.

C.   Renaissance Style

By 1450 the innovations of Masaccio, Donatello, and Brunelleschi had produced a recognizable Renaissance style, nowhere more apparent than in Florence. For the middle period of the Renaissance, the greatest architect was Leon Battista Alberti. He continued Brunelleschi's technique of utilizing basic geometric forms according to Euclidean theorems. Alberti not only worked in monumental scale, but also transferred the new style to domestic scale. No sculptor of the middle period surpassed the artistic achievements of Donatello, but there were many painting masters. Piero della Francesca surpassed Masaccio's study of linear perspective, possibly under the influence of Alberti's geometric studies in architecture. Sandro Botticelli introduced a greater sense of romanticism and emotion than the more rigorously geometric painters. Better known still was Leonardo da Vinci. A master of composition (*The Last Supper*) and portraiture (*La Gioconda* or the *Mona Lisa*), Leonardo also was a master of scientific speculation.

D.   Michelangelo

The most complete master of the Renaissance was Michelangelo Buonarroti—sculptor, painter, poet, and architect. A son of a wealthy Florentine family, Michelangelo underwent the customary training as an apprentice in an artistic shop patronized by Lorenzo de' Medici. His period of apprenticeship, two years, was remarkably brief. During his studies he may have been influenced by Neoplatonist philosophers who also enjoyed Lorenzo de' Medici's patronage. Following his apprenticeship, Michelangelo embarked on a career that took him first to Rome and then back to Florence. Between 1496 and 1504 he created two masterpieces of sculpture, the *Pietà* and *David*. The expressiveness and majesty of the two works guaranteed the artist's fame. A third work, the paintings covering the ceiling of the Sistine Chapel in Rome, established Michelangelo as a painter as well as a sculptor. In some ways the most impressive achievement of the Sistine Chapel was Michelangelo's ability to make the rounded surface of the ceiling appear flat when the frescoes were viewed from the floor. Michelangelo's masterpieces continued throughout his career, but the crowning glory of his life was the completion of the dome for St. Peter's Cathedral, the seat of St. Peter's grave. The building of the dome was considered an architectural impossibility, but Michelangelo solved the load-bearing problems and integrated the structure into the already completed base of the cathedral. Renaissance art was an expression of the society that was responsible for its creation. It merged the renewed taste for classical models with the remnants of medieval art. A contemporary observer was able to list over two hundred major artists of the period.

IV. Renaissance Ideals

A. Introduction

Renaissance thought was embodied in the scholarly approach called humanism. Like Renaissance art, humanism entailed the synthesis of classical literary forms into the educational system. Those responsible for the recovery and interpretation of classical texts were referred to as humanists. While humanism did include topics that could be considered secular in nature and did often dwell on the accomplishments of man, there was nothing antireligious in the humanistic curriculum. Many humanists applied the study of classical languages to ecclesiastical texts, including the Bible.

B. Humanists and the Liberal Arts

At the heart of humanistic education was the study of ancient texts, particularly Greek works. After the fall of Constantinople to the Turks in 1453, Italy became the center of Greek studies. Humanism also departed from Scholasticism in the points of emphasis within the curriculum. Humanists placed importance on grammar, rhetoric, moral philosophy, and history. Of the ancient authors, Cicero was most favored as a model for humanistic studies. Petrarch was responsible for the elevation of Cicero to the humanistic pedestal. Petrarch's most important successor, Leonardo Bruni, concentrated on the study of the texts of the two major Greek philosophers, Plato and Aristotle. Bruni was one of the founders of the influential Florentine Platonic Academy. Lorenzo Valla was famed for his study of philology, the study of the origin of words. Rigorously utilizing the humanistic study of philology, Valla invalidated the papacy's claims to secular authority in Italy by proving the so-called Donation of Constantine a forgery. Humanists tended to be political activists. They intended that humanistic studies should have a positive bearing on contemporary life. Leon Battista Alberti wrote a tract proposing proper family lifestyles in the urban setting. Even more influential was the work of Baldesar Castiglione. In *The Courtier* Castiglione defined the qualities necessary for the successful member of the ruling elite. *The Courtier* was both a book of etiquette and political science.

C. Machiavelli and Politics

In *The Prince* Niccolò Machiavelli portrayed the ideal characteristics of a ruling prince in Renaissance Italy. His work has been interpreted as the blueprint for power politics without regard to public benefit. The son of a relatively poor lawyer, Machiavelli received a humanistic education before entering public service in the Florentine government. He served primarily as a diplomat until his dismissal from office and subsequent banishment. In exile he composed his literary works, including *The Prince*. Machiavelli's dissection of the proper use of power is based on classical models drawn from history. It is entirely secular in mood. The sole concern of the ruler is maintaining power without reference to ethics. Rulers were advised to conquer, murder, and deceive in order to restore the ancient empire.

V.   The Politics of the Italian City-States

A.   Introduction

The Italian peninsula was dotted with city-states. The economic supremacy of the cities was a result of their position astride the trade routes between East and West. They supplied manufactured goods to the less urbanized regions of western Europe, while their agricultural hinterlands yielded adequate supplies of foodstuffs. Each state was a political entity that competed politically and militarily with its neighbors.

B.   The Five Powers

Five political units dominated the affairs of Italy. In the far south, hereditary monarchs ruled the kingdom of Naples, including the island of Sicily. In the middle of the fifteenth century, the kingdom fell to the Spanish monarchs of Aragon. Just north of the kingdom of Naples lay the Papal States, technically ruled from Rome. Within the Papal States were numerous semi-independent cities seeking to distance themselves from ecclesiastical government. The last three political powers were city-states of northern Italy. Florence and Venice were republics. The former was inland. The latter was a maritime republic, dependent on sea power, and only later developing dominance over its landlocked neighbors. The last of the group was Milan, governed by a single aristocratic family. Until 1450, the political affairs of the Italian peninsula were chaotic. Foreign invasions, internal insurrections and political rivalries, and inter-city warfare destroyed any semblance of order. After the middle of the fifteenth century, internal order was achieved through the development of increasingly centralized governments. The republics saw the emergence of powerful elites that gained control over the electoral processes. In Milan, Francesco Sforza established a new military government. The succession of the Aragonese to the throne of Naples brought order in the South. Finally, the end of the Great Schism allowed the popes to restore their authority within the Papal States. Restoration of internal order led to the creation of a diplomatic balance of power within the peninsula. Sforza's overthrow of the Visconti in Milan led to the Peace of Lodi and the alliance of Milan with Florence and of Venice with Naples.

C.   Venice: A Seaborne Empire

Venice's prosperity was based on its military and commercial control of the seas. From the tenth century, Venice enjoyed a privileged position in Byzantine trade. All of the lucrative trade coming into the city from the east had to be carried on Venetian galleys. The republican government controlled all merchant contracts in such a way that many, rather than a few, prospered. Venetian government was also intended to distribute power among many. A strictly regulated oligarchy, power was restricted to those families able to secure membership in the Great Council. From the approximately 2,500 men who were members of the Great Council, all public officers were chosen.

Terms of public service were brief, and even the highest offices were distributed evenly among all members of the Great Council. Venice was able to create an enormous overseas empire in the East along the lines of its trade routes to the Byzantine Empire. In the fifteenth century, Venice began to extend its control to the west into the Italian peninsula. In part, the creation of a land empire was to balance the loss of eastern trade associated with the fall of Constantinople.

D.   Florence: Spinning Cloth into Gold

The Florentine economy was based on the commercial successes of its numerous banking houses and on the industrial capacity of its woolen crafts. The calamities of the mid-fourteenth century ended prosperity for many banking families and for the cloth industry. Eligibility for the Florentine government depended on guild membership. As the number of guild masters was few, the government in Florence, as in Venice, was an oligarchic republic. Leaders among Florentine families were able to create powerful factions and to control access to public office. In the fourteenth and fifteenth centuries, the Medici family was able to secure domination of the Florentine government. The Medici were a powerful banking family whose members were closely associated as patrons with the cultural revival of the Renaissance. The most famous of the family was Lorenzo the Magnificent. Himself a product of a humanistic education, Lorenzo excelled at diplomacy. He was able to maintain the balance of power in the Italian peninsula, although his concentration on political affairs permitted his banking house to collapse. In the long run, the success of the Medici political faction corrupted the sense of republicanism in Florence.

E.   The End of Italian Hegemony, 1450–1527

During the Renaissance, Italy enjoyed a political, cultural, and economic hegemony over western Europe. The political empires of the five major states of Italy were tenuous. They were immediately threatened by the expansion of the Ottoman Empire under Mehmed II. Conquerors of the Byzantine Empire, the Ottomans rapidly extended their control to the Balkan peninsula and to Greece. The Ottomans posed a most direct threat to the Venetians, who lost their seaborne empire in the East. Despite the Ottoman challenge, the Italian states were unable to overcome their individual differences. Instead, they plunged into an internecine conflict that destroyed the equilibrium of political power in Italy. Wars between the Italian states brought foreign intervention. Charles VIII of France in alliance with Milan successfully conquered most of northern Italy. In response, the defeated powers brought in Spain and the Holy Roman Emperor to offset the influence of the French. The myth of Italian power was destroyed in the Italian Wars.

TIMELINE

Insert the following events into the timeline. This should help you to compare important historical events chronologically.

publication of *The Prince*	fall of Constantinople
Wars of Italy	Peace of Lodi
publication of *The Courtier*	completion of Michelangelo's *David*

- 1453
- 1454
- 1494–1529
- 1504
- 1513
- 1528

TERMS, PEOPLE, EVENTS

The following terms, people, and events are important to your understanding of the chapter. Define each one.

Renaissance	Petrarch	Brunelleschi
Donatello	Masaccio	Leon Battista Alberti
Sandro Botticelli	Piero della Francesca	Leonardo da Vinci
Michelangelo	Lorenzo de' Medici	humanism
Pico della Mirandola	Lorenzo Valla	Leonardo Bruni
philology	Baldesar Castiglione	Niccolò Machiavelli
The Courtier	*The Prince*	Naples
Milan	Florence	Venice
Papal States	doge	Francesco Sforza
condottieri	Peace of Lodi	oligarchy
Signoria	Cosimo de' Medici	Mehmed II
Wars of Italy		

MAP EXERCISE

The following exercise is intended to clarify the geophysical environment and the spatial relationships among the important objects and places mentioned in the chapter. Locate the following places on the map.

kingdom of Naples   Milan   Florence
Rome   Papal States   Venice

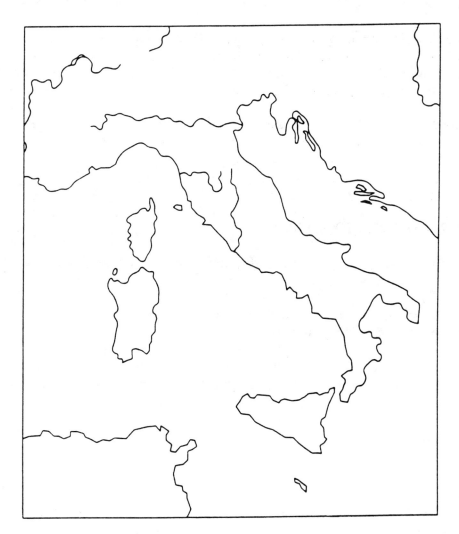

1. What geographical features help to determine the political fragmentation of Italy? [Hint: Locate the mountain ranges and river systems of Italy.]

2. How did access to the sea affect the political orientation of the major Italian powers?

MAKING CONNECTIONS

The following questions are intended to emphasize important ideas within the chapter.

1. What was the political culture of Renaissance Italy? What defined the economy of the Renaissance cities? Define the social structure.

2. Discuss the artistic achievement of the Renaissance in the areas of architecture, sculpture, and painting.

3. Define humanism. What were the humanists' most important achievements?

4. What were the five major political units of the Italian peninsula? What was the political structure of each of them?

5. What impact did the advance of the Ottomans have on Italy?

6. How did the Wars of Italy destroy Italian hegemony?

PUTTING LARGER CONCEPTS TOGETHER

The following questions test your ability to summarize the major conclusions of the chapter.

1. How did the peculiar social, political, and economic status of the Italian city-states foster the environment that led to the cultural genius of the Renaissance?

2. Was the Italian Renaissance new, or did it simply restate what was already present in Western civilization? Consider both the political and cultural orientation of the Italian city-states.

SELF-TEST OF FACTUAL INFORMATION

1. Which of the following statements concerning the Renaissance is *not* correct?

    a. The word *Renaissance* means "rebirth".
    b. Petrarch was among the first to differentiate the new age from two earlier ones: the classical period and the Dark Ages.
    c. Renaissance thinking emphasized humanity and the classical world.
    d. It is easy to define the moment at which the Middle Ages ended and the Renaissance began.

2. Renaissance cities

    a. were small in both area and population.
    b. typically numbered over one million inhabitants.
    c. were organized around the ownership of land.
    d. diminished the differences in wealth between the rich and poor.

3. Which of the following statements concerning Renaissance art is *not* accurate?

    a. Techniques or experiments in Renaissance art owed much to the social context in which they were produced.
    b. Artists were closely tied to the crafts and trades of urban society.
    c. Art in the Renaissance was produced by skilled tradespeople.
    d. Unlike most craftsmen in Renaissance towns, artists did not undergo a period of apprenticeship in a master's shop.

4. Who was the author of *On Building*?

    a. Niccolò Machiavelli
    b. Leon Battista Alberti
    c. Sandro Botticelli
    d. Michelangelo

5. Humanism made its most impressive contributions in

    a. science.
    b. philosophy.
    c. recovery of ancient texts.
    d. religion.

6. What was the purpose of *The Courtier*?

    a. to prescribe characteristics that would make the ideal state servant
    b. to detail the inner workings of power politics
    c. to define the nature of Renaissance art
    d. to describe the concept of geometric perspective

7. What was Machiavelli's objective in writing *The Prince*?

    a. to incorporate ethical considerations into political decisions
    b. to reestablish Italian rule and place government on a stable basis
    c. to introduce the governmental experience of Spain into Italy
    d. to exclude humanism from the study of politics

8. Which of the following was *not* a reason for the dominance of the Italian city-states in the Christian world?

    a. Their geographical position favored the exchange of goods and resources between East and West.
    b. There was a constant need for goods in the Holy Roman Empire that only Italy could supply.
    c. The city-states were agriculturally self-sufficient.
    d. The homogeneity of political structure among all of the city-states permitted them to cooperate easily.

9. Which of the following was *not* a reason for Venice's turn to the West in the fifteenth century?

    a. exhaustion as a result of the Genoese wars
    b. the threat of Ottoman expansion in the East
    c. competition with the Portuguese over the control of spices
    d. the establishment of a centralized monarchy in Venice

10. What city-state began the Wars of Italy by inviting France to invade the peninsula?

    a. Florence
    b. Milan
    c. Venice
    d. Naples

Chapter 12

The European Empires

OUTLINE

I.   Ptolemy's World

The cosmos of sixteenth century Europeans was still defined by the scheme created by Ptolemy in the second century. The world was perceived as round with landmasses corresponding to Europe, Africa, and Asia roughly distributed from West to East. Land area was greater than the portions of the world covered by seas.

II.   European Encounters

A.   Introduction

The sixteenth century was an age of discovery. A number of reasons created interest in exploratory voyages. Seafaring technology improved, Ottoman expansion cut off the traditional routes to eastern markets while demands for goods of the East continued to grow. Lacking export goods, western consumers were forced to purchase eastern luxuries with bullion. The need for greater supplies of bullion also stimulated exploration.

B.   A Passage to India

The first nation to initiate exploratory voyages was Portugal. Early voyages charted the waters of western Africa where bullion and black slaves were the primary products. By the beginning of the sixteenth century, Portuguese explorers had rounded the Cape of Good Hope and established trade routes to the spice markets of India and Indonesia. The Portuguese commercial empire also extended to Brazil in the New World. Fortifications and garrisons defended strategic discoveries and trade routes.

C.   *Mundus Novus*

While Portuguese efforts were concentrated on the spice trade with the East, the Spanish devoted their attention to the New World. A late starter in the establishment of routes to the East, Spain determined to gamble on a western route to the spice markets. With the support of Ferdinand and Isabella, the Genoese adventurer Christopher Columbus voyaged westward to the New World. When potential conflict between Spain and Portugal over the new territories seemed likely, the papacy allotted Brazil to the Portuguese and all other lands to the Spanish in the Treaty of Tordesillas. Full realization of the global arrangement of the new discoveries was only achieved after the circumnavigation of the globe by the crew of Ferdinand Magellan. The voyage destroyed hopes for a practical new route to the spice markets of Asia and forced the Spanish to concentrate on the imperial potential of the New World.

D.   The Spanish Conquests

Under the Spanish military commander Hernando Cortés, the conquest of the New World began. Military venturers were given control over land they conquered in return for attempts to Christianize the native population and to find marketable commodities, especially bullion, for Spanish markets. Native populations were ruthlessly subdued and converted to semi-free agricultural laborers. Hernando Cortés undertook the conquest of the Aztec empire of central Mexico. With a force of only six hundred men, Cortés defeated the Aztecs under their emperor Montezuma II. Superior technology, firearms, and cavalry (horses were unknown to the Aztecs) permitted Cortés to defeat overwhelming numerical superiority. The Spanish conquest decimated the native population. In 1531 Francisco Pizarro repeated Cortés' success against the Peruvian empire of the Incas. The conquest of the Incas proved the wisdom of the conquistadors in extending the dominions of Spain. Huge supplies of bullion were discovered in the Incan empire and exported to Europe. In return, the Spanish sent colonists, including women, to "civilize" the New World.

E.   The Legacy of the Encounters

By the seventeenth century the New World had been yoked to an international system based on the triangular trade between Europe, Africa, Asia, and the Americas. Whether in the East or the New World, imperial motivation could be summarized under the westerners' search for "gold, God, and glory." Conquistadors and explorers became popular heroes celebrated in story and song. Despite real natural hazards and imagined dangers, the discoverers carved out new routes and markets. Some successes could be attributed to European technological superiority. Better navigational devices, ship design, and chart making made long-distance sea travel possible. Military advantages through the use of battle-tested gunpowder and cannon insured Western victories over less well-armed peoples. Europe also began to interpret the home civilizations in terms of the newly discovered ones. Essayists became interested in the viewpoint of native Americans, but the concern of intellectuals was insufficient to halt the processes of debasement and enslavement that followed colonization. Intentional and unintentional destruction of native cultures was an invariable concomitant of discovery and conquest.

III.   Europe in 1500

A.   Introduction

The voyages of discovery and conquest coincided with the development of more centralized nation states, the New Monarchies, in western Europe.

B.   Eastern Boundaries

Three empires created the eastern European boundaries. To the southeast, the khanates of the Mongol empire marked the borders of Europe. Once a single political unit under the great founding khans, the Mongol territories were now divided into smaller states. To the south, the newly emergent Ottoman Empire succeeded to the lands once ruled by the Byzantines. The Balkan peninsula served as a buffer zone between the Ottoman territories and the West. To the northeast, the Russian

116

principalities—notably those centered on Moscow and Kiev—established the limits of European culture. In the latter principalities, the borders between East and West were less absolute. Technically within European boundaries but on the periphery of European political affairs were the lands bordering the Baltic Sea. The Scandinavian nations (Sweden, Denmark, and Norway), the lands of the Teutonic Knights, and Poland-Lithuania surrounded the northern inland sea. Territorially distinct but united to Poland-Lithuania through a single dynasty, the Jagiellons, were Hungary and Bohemia. Bohemia, in particular, was drawn into the European arena as a part of the Holy Roman Empire. Wealth on the eastern frontier of Europe was based on Baltic fisheries, Russian forests, and Hungarian and Bohemian mines. Ethnically, the region was a diverse mixture of German colonists, Asian conquerors, and native Slavic peoples.

C.   Central Europe

All of central Europe was taken up by the ill-defined mass of the Germanic or Holy Roman Empire. The extreme decentralization of the empire left central Europe a jumble of competing political jurisdictions—principalities, imperial cities, and episcopal states. The greater states lay in the eastern portions of the Holy Roman Empire. The western half of the empire was completely fragmented into smaller political units. At the mouth of the Rhine lay the Low Countries, still among the wealthiest regions of western Europe. The Holy Roman Empire was rich in resources. It possessed fertile agricultural regions producing grain and the Mediterranean luxury products, wine and olive oil. The European mining industry was centered here. Finally, the Hanseatic League controlled a vast commercial system.

D.   The West

The western borders of Europe were taken up by the Iberian Peninsula, France, and the British Isles. During the Middle Ages, Muslims controlled Spain. Muslim domination came to an end in 1492, when the united Christian kingdoms of Castile and Aragon completed the *reconquista*. In addition to Castile and Aragon, Portugal existed on the Atlantic shoreline. France, like Spain, had ports on the Mediterranean and the Atlantic. France was bordered on the east by the Holy Roman Empire, and England lay only a few miles off the northwestern coast. France enjoyed one of the most prosperous agricultural systems in Europe. The British islands included England, Wales, Scotland, and Ireland. Of these, England was the most prosperous with a successful and varied agricultural system. England also developed a woolen cloth industry. Wales and Scotland were less populated than England. Difficult climates and geography limited the economic development of both. Ireland had a better climate for agriculture, but Ireland, too, was less populated than England. The political shape of Europe was still in its formative stages.

IV.   The Formation of States

A.   Introduction

In the mid-fifteenth century, there were many factors that made the creation of great states difficult, if not impossible. Distance was the enemy of centralization. Transportation and communication systems were too primitive to permit close contact with far-flung parts of huge empires. Larger regions also tended to be fragmented culturally with different languages and political customs creating distinct regionalism. There were mundane political reasons for smaller states. Inheritance varied from one place to another. In some regions it was still customary to divide the estate among all heirs.

France excluded women from the royal line. Uncertainty in the principles of succession commonly implied continual struggles over inheritance and legitimacy. The aristocracy, imperial cities, and the Church also sought to frustrate the creation of centralized monarchies in which their own powers would diminish. The advance of military technology, however, gave princes the power to subdue some of their weaker neighbors. The process of centralization began to take place.

B.   Eastern Configurations

At the outset of the sixteenth century, the most successful program of centralization in eastern Europe had been undertaken in the principality of Muscovy. External threats, such as the Mongols and the Byzantine Empire, had diminished. Indeed, Moscow and its prince became heirs to Constantinople as head of the Orthodox Church. The most successful monarch, Ivan III the Great, had no internal competitors for the throne. Ivan's successors maintained his military and political successes. Expansion finally came to an end under Ivan IV, the Terrible. The principality failed to establish a Baltic port after many years of warfare with Poland-Lithuania. Ivan IV also was responsible for social changes in Muscovy. Muscovite society consisted of three estates: the boyars (the old hereditary nobility), the knights or military service class whose lands were received from the prince, and the agricultural workers. Ivan attempted to diminish the authority of the boyars. Ivan reduced the boyars' control over land, decimated their numbers through trials and suppression, and pushed them down into the ranks of the military service class. The removal of the boyars effectively eliminated the Russian aristocracy and paved the way for centralization. Ivan created administrative offices to deal with all phases of local government. Russian agricultural peasants were ruthlessly ground down into servile status. Poland-Lithuania experienced fragmentation rather than centralization during the same period. Originally the states of Poland, Lithuania, Bohemia, and Hungary were united under a single family. The accession of the Jagiellons was accomplished through concessions to local aristocracies, not through conquest. As a result, all of the territories split into separate jurisdictions in the course of the sixteenth century. The failure of centralization in eastern Europe was due to many reasons. Unlike Muscovy, there were powerful external rivals—Muscovy, itself, and the Ottomans. There were also important internal forces preventing centralization. The regional aristocracy of the eastern frontier was not eliminated. The Habsburgs also challenged the Jagiellons for supremacy in the region.

C.   The Western Powers

England's status as an island gave it immunity from external attack. Factionalism among powerful aristocratic families led by two cadet branches of the royal family led to prolonged civil wars, the Wars of the Roses. Eventually the two cadet families, Lancaster and York, were destroyed. The throne fell to Henry Tudor, a distant relative of the Lancastrians. In order to centralize England, it was necessary to limit the power of the aristocracy and create solvency for the Crown. The new aristocracy of state service replaced the old feudal aristocracy. By 1525 there were only two English dukes left alive. Royal revenues depended on the income from estates and from customs. Parliament limited the king's ability to tax the real property of the aristocracy. Thus administrative reform focused on efficiency in running royal estates and in collecting taxes on commerce. The resources available to the Crown remained limited until Henry VIII confiscated all Church property in England. To deal with the financial bonanza, one of Henry VIII's chief ministers, Thomas Cromwell, created an administrative system composed of separate departments dedicated to specific tasks. All departments were coordinated through the Privy Council, a small body of trusted advisors that functioned as the executive. Cromwell also began the political process of controlling the work of

Parliament through the establishment of royal factions.

France became a centralized state only by overcoming significant centrifugal tendencies. Provincialism, a powerful aristocracy, aggressive external neighbors, and the size of the French state all militated against centralization. France's first challenge was the successful conclusion of the Hundred Years' War and the related independence of the dukes of Burgundy. Controlling virtually the entire eastern frontier of France, Burgundy posed an enormous threat to a unified France. Thanks to a Swiss revolution against Burgundian influence, the French were able to defeat Burgundy and annex many of the Burgundian territories to France. Under King Louis XI, the French nobility was reduced in influence. Through marriage alliances and simple exhaustion of aristocratic heirs, Louis gained control of most of the major estates of France. Only the Low Countries passed out of his control. Virtually continuous warfare strengthened the principles of royal taxation in France beyond those of any other European state. Similarly, the long years of war created a national army—raised, supplied, and paid for by the state. Taxation and militarization marked the beginning of centralization in France.

The marriage of Ferdinand of Aragon and Isabella of Castile made possible the unification of Spain. Although the two crowns were united, Aragon jealously regarded its traditions of limited royal authority. In some ways, the creation of Spain was a product of the *reconquista*, the successful campaigns to free the Iberian Peninsula from the influence of North African Muslims. The process was finally completed in 1492. Militarization, as in France, was the first step in centralization. Most conquered territories were handed over to Castile where they were used to reward helpful aristocrats. As a side-product of the *reconquista*, Spanish Jews were harassed. In 1492 the Jewish population of Spain was expelled. Ferdinand and Isabella were succeeded by their grandson Charles V, heir to Castile, Aragon, Naples, the Low Countries, and the Holy Roman Empire. Forced to govern such a disparate group of states, Charles depended on Spain for the development of a centralized administrative system of councils. The resultant bureaucracy allowed Charles to be absent for long periods of time. Charles' real success in the unification of Spain, however, was a result of aggressive foreign policy. He carried on war with the Ottoman Empire, secured Aragonese possession of Naples, and pressed the development of Spanish colonies in the New World.

V.   The Dynastic Struggles

A.   Introduction

The development of increasingly centralized states and foreign colonies led inevitably to prolonged warfare between the aspiring monarchs. The sixteenth century was devoted to imperial wars.

B.   Power and Glory

Wars were fought in the sixteenth century for the benefit of princes. Conflict was essentially dynastic. As states became more organized, they were better able to practice the arts of war. Bullion from the New World and state taxation permitted the hiring of professional soldiers and the purchase of new technology. Improvements in communication and transportation made long-distance warfare more feasible. Finally, personal ambitions played a role in the growth of militarism. Charles V of Spain and the Holy Roman Empire, Francis I of France, and Henry VIII of England were bitter rivals and competitors.

119

C. The Italian Wars

The theater for the wars, especially those pitting the French against the Habsburgs of Spain and the Holy Roman Empire, was Italy. Constant warfare between major Italian city-states offered opportunities for intervention. The French first interceded on the side of Milan in 1494. Naples was a bone of contention between the royal houses of France and Spain. Conflict between Habsburg and Valois monarchs broke out in 1515, again over Milan. Henry VIII of England also sought to play a role in these conflicts. Eventually allied to the Habsburg emperor, Henry VIII launched a series of abortive invasions of France. While the English failed to gain much, the emperor made use of the distraction to push his advantage in northern Italy. At the battle of Pavia, Charles V actually captured Francis I. In the Treaty of Madrid of 1526, Francis I was forced to cede Burgundy to the Habsburgs and to recognize the Spanish conquest of Navarre and Aragon's rights to Naples. The French king immediately renounced the treaty and prepared for renewed war. New alliances were created against the Habsburg possessions. England and the Ottoman Empire joined France. The combination proved too much for Charles V. Conflict was finally halted by the Treaty of Cateau-Cambrésis. Six decades of conflict bankrupted both France and Spain financially and in terms of human resources. Exhausted, Charles V divided the Habsburg empire between his brother (the Holy Roman Empire) and his son (Spain, the Low Countries, and Naples). The emperor abdicated and retired to a monastery in 1555.

TIMELINE

Insert the following events into the timeline. This should help you to compare important historical events chronologically.

beginning of reign of Ivan IV the Terrible
Cortés begins conquest of Aztecs
unification of crowns of Castile and Aragon

Dias enters Indian Ocean for first time
Treaty of Cateau-Cambrésis
Treaty of Tordesillas

⊢	1479
⊢	1487
⊢	1494
⊢	1519
⊢	1533
⊢	1559

TERMS, PEOPLE, EVENTS

The following terms, people, and events are important to your understanding of the chapter. Define each one.

Prince Henry the Navigator
Alfonso de Albuquerque
Vasco Núñez de Balboa
Muscovy
boyars
Jagiellon dynasty
Louis XI
aide
reconquista
Francis I of France
Treaty of Cateau-Cambrésis

Bartolomeu Dias
Christopher Columbus
Hernando Cortés
Ivan III, the Great
Michael Romanov
Henry VII Tudor
taille
Ferdinand of Aragon
conversos
Valois dynasty

Vasco da Gama
Ferdinand Magellan
Francisco Pizarro
Ivan IV, the Terrible
Poland-Lithuania
Thomas Cromwell
gabelle
Isabella of Castile
Emperor Charles V
Habsburg Empire

MAP EXERCISE

The following exercise is intended to clarify the geophysical environment and the spatial relationships among the important objects and places mentioned in the chapter. Locate the following places on the map.

Cape of Good Hope	Brazil	Ceylon
Indonesia	Tenochtitlán	Inca Empire

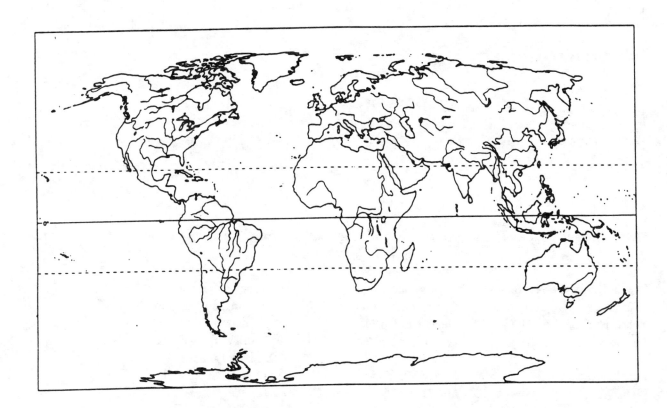

1.   What was the geographical emphasis of the Portuguese colonial empire? What was the geographical emphasis of the Spanish colonial empire? What were the primary products of each?

MAKING CONNECTIONS

The following questions are intended to emphasize important ideas within the chapter.

1. What factors led to European exploration and discovery? What nation led the process? What made the Europeans virtually invincible against the defenses of indigenous peoples? What was the impact of the discoveries on the European concept of self?

2. What defined the boundaries of Europe in 1500?

3. What factors slowed the formation of states in Europe?

4. What was the political configuration of eastern Europe to 1650? What was the political configuration of western Europe? Which part of Europe featured more centralized states?

5. Why did the formation of states lead almost immediately to prolonged warfare?

PUTTING LARGER CONCEPTS TOGETHER

The following questions test your ability to summarize the major conclusions of the chapter.

1. By 1500 Europe was in the process of forming more centralized states and of expanding their dominion beyond Europe. How were these two developments related? Is it true that the more centralized states were responsible for exploration and discovery? How did this second episode of colonialism compare to the first (the Crusades)?

2. By the sixteenth century, how did the concept of empire fare in Europe? What accounts for the dominance of political particularism? Can it be related to the process of state formation?

SELF-TEST OF FACTUAL INFORMATION

1. Which of the following was *not* a cause of the European explorations?

    a. Magyar invasions of eastern Europe
    b. technological advances that made longer sea voyages possible
    c. Ottoman expansion that threatened traditional trade routes to the East
    d. European demand for Eastern spices that sparked demand for new routes to the Orient

2. At the turn of the sixteenth century, Portugal

    a. overextended its supply lines and fell out of the race for colonization.
    b. became one of the trading capitals of the world.
    c. became involved in a costly war with the Ottoman Empire.
    d. joined with England and Spain to ensure European domination of the East.

3. The Treaty of Tordesillas settled claims to the New World between what two countries?

    a. England and Spain
    b. France and Portugal
    c. Spain and Portugal
    d. Spain and France

4. Which of the following was *not* a state forming the eastern boundary of Europe?

    a. Mongol khanates
    b. Ottoman Empire
    c. Muscovy and Kiev
    d. Holy Roman Empire

5. Which of the following was *not* a hindrance to the formation of large states in Europe?

    a. rivals with strong claims to legitimacy
    b. transportation and communications
    c. the European nobility
    d. dynastic marriage

6. What was the largest European political unit at the beginning of the sixteenth century?

    a. France
    b. Spain
    c. Muscovy
    d. Sweden

7. Henry VII did all of the following to bring order to England *except*

   a. put an end to dynastic instability.
   b. rule without Parliament.
   c. introduce efficient management of royal estates.
   d. create a new peerage.

8. What king was most closely associated in the fifteenth century with the consolidation of the French state?

   a. Francis I
   b. Henry II
   c. Robert II
   d. Louis XI

9. Which of the following was *not* an outcome of the *reconquista* in Spain?

   a. Ferdinand was recognized as the undisputed king of a united Spain after Isabella's death.
   b. The Moors finally lost their last stronghold in Spain in 1492.
   c. The *reconquista* helped to create a national identity for the Christian peoples of Spain.
   d. The idea of a holy war led to the expulsion of the Jews and attacks on the *conversos*.

10. The primary sixteenth-century venue for the conflict between the Valois and the Habsburgs was

    a. Germany.
    b. France.
    c. Spain.
    d. Italy.

Chapter 13

The Reform of Religion

OUTLINE

I. *Sola Scriptura*

In the sixteenth century the Bible left the church and cloister and became the common reading material for homes all over Europe. The principles of humanism were applied to biblical studies. Commentaries and interpretations of Scripture became popular among the general population. The new emphasis on the Bible as the basis of religious studies was typical of the renewal of spirituality found in European culture.

II. The Intellectual Reformation

A. Introduction

Religious reform, whether Protestant or Catholic, was a common element of the sixteenth-century intellectual tradition. The introduction of the printing press permitted the distribution of new ideas throughout society.

B. The Print Revolution

Printing developed out of a series of related technological advances. Gradually, paper replaced sheepskin, or vellum, as the primary material for the recording of copyists' work. Metalsmiths also perfected the use of moveable type to allow the mechanical reproduction of manuscripts, which was much more rapid and accurate than hand copying. The best known of the early printers was Johannes Gutenberg. Because of the expense of paper and skilled labor necessary for the production of metal type, printing remained expensive. Printing spread rapidly from Germany to neighboring countries. It quickly revolutionized education, scientific study, and legal training. The ease of repetition also standardized language and created an international community of literate scholars.

C. Christian Humanism

Humanism, as defined in the Italian Renaissance, benefited from the print revolution. In northern Europe, humanistic techniques of text reproduction and evaluation were applied to religious documents. Christian humanists wished to better society, including women, through education based on examination and critique of religious texts. The humanistic approach to Christian education began to diverge from that of the Catholic Church. Scholasticism remained the principal form of ecclesiastical training.

D.   The Humanist Movement

Humanist scholars criticized the Church for intellectual crudity and superstition. The two great humanists, Desiderius Erasmus and Thomas More, both questioned the authenticity of relics. Humanists were not isolated, but corresponded across state boundaries. The New Monarchs tended to support and protect humanists from ecclesiastical interference. Christian humanists concentrated on the translation of religious texts. The Polyglot Bible, produced in Spain in 1522, offered comparative versions of the Scriptures in Hebrew, Greek, and Latin.

E.   The Wit of Erasmus

The man most closely associated with Christian humanism is Desiderius Erasmus. Educated in a lay brotherhood, the Brothers of Common Life, Erasmus set out on an international career that took him to France and then England. He published two popular works of humanistic criticism, *In Praise of Folly* and *Adages*. After studying Greek, Erasmus offered a critical edition of the New Testament, followed shortly by a new Latin translation of the same. Like most humanists, Erasmus had little patience for Scholasticism and the traditional forms of education in the Church. He hoped that the practice of Christian education could be extended to the masses.

III.   The Lutheran Reformation

A.   Introduction

The Church survived the late medieval crises of the Babylonian captivity and the Schism to reemerge as a powerful factor in sixteenth-century politics. The popes in Rome survived the Italian Wars and maintained their independence. Despite the majesty of the Church, many demanded reforms of abuses—inordinate wealth of clergymen, ignorant priests, pluralism, and sale of Church offices.

B.   The Spark of Reform

Generally speaking, sixteenth-century Europe was experiencing a revival of religious fervor. Religious pilgrimage sites were active; ecclesiastical endowments rose. As religious demands for reform grew, so did demands for traditional religious services. One short cut invented by the Church was the sale of indulgences, which replaced confession and penance with a (hopefully) pious contribution. In return for a monetary payment, Christians could dip into the treasury of merit and receive dispensations for their own sins or those of their loved ones. The papacy claimed a monopoly on the sale of indulgences through licensed agents. The sale of indulgences to fund the rebuilding of St. Peter's Basilica in Rome in 1517 provoked a revolutionary response. Although ostensibly a strictly religious question, the furor over the sale of indulgences was, at least in part, a competition between two German lords in possession of relics suitable for the indulgence business. Into the dispute stepped Martin Luther, a professor of theology at Wittenberg University. He attacked the theological basis for indulgences in a series of 95 theses or arguments. Luther's attack on indulgences was rapidly translated into German and received wide dissemination throughout Germany. The assault on indulgences as ineffective nostrums for the superstitious met with the approval of Christian humanists, but earned the enmity of the papacy who depended on the income from the sale to rebuild St. Peter's.

C.   Martin Luther's Faith

Martin Luther began his ecclesiastical career as an Augustinian monk and priest. He continued his studies at the universities at Erfurt and Wittenberg. In 1512 he became a professor at the latter school. He was a renowned teacher and debater. Luther suffered, however, from inner doubts concerning the safety of his soul. Through his studies of the Bible, Luther resolved his doubt and, in the process, created a theological revolution. Following a critical review of the Pauline Epistles, Luther developed a series of fundamental beliefs. Justification, or salvation, came only from faith, not good works. All that anyone needed to know concerning religion could be found in the Bible, the sole authority for all spiritual matters. All men and women who had achieved faith were on an equal footing, and no man or woman could hold supernatural powers over another. All men were equally priests. Each of Luther's fundamental beliefs challenged the traditional doctrines of the Church. Justification by faith made the works of the Church—particularly the sacraments—useless. *Sola scriptura,* or the Bible as sole authority, struck at the collective authority of interpretation and regulation, including the canon law. The priesthood of all believers destroyed the superiority of all clerics. Luther's arguments reached a population ready to receive them. The concept of faith alone alleviated the oppressive burdens of confession, penance, and indulgence placed on Christians by the Church. His emphasis on the Bible echoed the concerns of the humanists and was fueled by the printing revolution. Luther's call for a spiritual elite fulfilled the desires of Germans for independence from an Italian clergy. Luther, himself, did not realize the impact of his theology.

D.   Lutheranism

Both the papacy and the Holy Roman Emperor assaulted Luther's theology. Their attacks led Luther to increasingly radical statements including a condemnation of the papacy and general Church councils. In his *Address to the Christian Nobility of the German Nation,* Luther requested that princes in Germany initiate religious reform without the consent of the Church. In response, the pope excommunicated Luther in 1521. Under external military and political pressures, neither pope nor emperor was free to dispose of Luther as they wished. In addition, the electoral prince of Saxony offered Luther protection within his domain. The reformer became an effective pamphleteer, publishing many works that were distributed throughout Europe. Luther's work attracted the support of additional German princes and the cities. To the princes of the fragmented territories of Germany, Luther's religion offered an opportunity to free themselves from papal taxation and interference. To the independent imperial cities, Luther's theology stressed the superiority of civil power over the Church and gave the city governments access to Church properties. The reform doctrine spread more rapidly in the cities as reformed clergy married and became townsmen. The reform message was particularly attractive to the middle orders of towns—the lesser merchants and craftsmen. Women also responded favorably to the reform movement. Some aristocratic women saw Lutheranism as another form of humanism. The doctrine of the equality of all Christians made women theoretically the equals of men, although the tradition of a male priesthood generally continued. Education for women improved. In contrast, because of the loss of the model of the female saints, Lutheranism tended toward male dominance in spiritual images. The decline of the convent deprived women of the only spiritual calling outside of marriage.

E.   The Spread of Lutheranism

Lutheranism spread rapidly throughout the decentralized Holy Roman Empire and from there to the states bordering the empire. Luther's students, printed materials, and merchants carried the reform message outward from Germany. Poland-Lithuania, the lands of the Teutonic Knights, and Prussia all established Lutheran churches. In Scandinavia, the monarchs of both Denmark and Sweden embraced the new reform religion. In each state it was seen as a means of expressing independence—in Denmark from the Roman church, in Sweden from Denmark. The earlier reform movement of Jan Hus prepared the way for Lutheranism in Bohemia, but the Hussites refused to take up the entirety of Luther's reform package and retained their separate identity as a Czech nationalist movement. In the Swiss towns, Luther's reforms were radicalized. The leader of the radical reform movement was Huldrych Zwingli of Zurich. Trained as a humanist, Zwingli sought to reestablish the purity of the ancient Church and reject the innovations of the medieval Church. Zwingli adopted the three foundation beliefs of Lutheranism and attacked the superstitious acts of Catholicism. He departed from Luther in reducing the significance of the mass as something done in remembrance of Christ's sacrifice rather than a literal reenactment of the sacrifice. In Swiss towns that adopted Zwingli's radical reform, the members of the new church became the civil government and created a theocracy.

IV.   The Protestant Reformation

A.   Introduction

Luther had attacked Catholicism, but had offered almost nothing as a constitutional structure to replace it. The Protestant reformers who came after Luther undertook the task of creating forms of ecclesiastical government for the new reformed churches.

B.   Geneva and Calvin

In the sixteenth century Geneva successfully freed itself from the overlordship of both the Catholic Church and the duke of Savoy. In 1536 the citizens of Geneva voted to embrace Protestantism on the model proposed by Zwingli. As a director for the newly accepted Protestantism, Geneva turned to John Calvin, a French lawyer and the author of *The Institutes of the Christian Religion*. Calvin's theology differed from Luther's primarily in the emphasis he placed on the doctrine of predestination—the belief that only some are predestined from the moment of creation for salvation. This permitted the formation of a spiritual and political elite of those sure of salvation—the "elect." The elect were divided into four governing offices: pastors to preach, doctors to develop theology, deacons to oversee the public institutions of Geneva, and elders to govern the population in matters of morality. Power to discipline offenders was vested in the consistory, a meeting of elders and pastors. With its strong constitutional structure, Calvinism was an effective evangelical church. It spread from Geneva to France and the Low Countries as well as parts of Germany.

C.   The English Reformation

The catalyst for the English Reformation was Henry VIII's need for a divorce. Without male heirs, Henry wanted to rid himself of his wife, Catherine of Aragon, and marry Anne Boleyn, a woman of his court. The papacy, heavily involved in the diplomacy of the Italian Wars, dragged its feet on the issue. Frustrated by delay, Henry VIII took the issue to Parliament. By statute, papal interference was denied. The case was handed over to the jurisdiction of the head of the English church, Archbishop of Canterbury Thomas Cranmer. Once the divorce was granted, Henry's chief minister, Thomas Cromwell, continued to construct a national church system independent of Rome. The king became head of the Anglican church, Catholic properties were confiscated, monasteries were dissolved, and a Lutheran form of church service was imposed. Nevertheless, the basic tenor of the Anglican church was close to Catholicism. The identity of church and state government in England meant that continued demands for reform were actually assaults on the state. In the reign of Edward VI, further reforms were initiated. The Anglican church under Thomas Cranmer adopted the Zwinglian interpretation of the Eucharist, services were conducted in English rather than Latin, and the priesthood was converted to a Protestant ministry. With the reforms, Catholics remaining in England began to be persecuted. There were even minor Catholic revolutions. Under Mary I, Catholicism was temporarily restored as the official religion in England. Archbishop Cranmer, the architect of the Anglican church, was burned at the stake as were some other leading Protestants. Other Protestants fled to the reformed communities of the Continent. Under Mary's successor, Elizabeth I, the Anglican church was brought back to Protestantism. While the restored Anglicanism continued to reflect deliberate moderation when compared to radical Protestantism, some Calvinist doctrines entered the Elizabethan church.

D.   The Reformation of the Radicals

Protestantism rapidly fragmented into various theologies, despite Luther's warnings concerning sectarianism. Various radical interpretations of scripture emerged, the most virulent of which were the groups called Anabaptists—those who baptized adults. Arising on the border of Switzerland and Germany, Anabaptists believed in an exclusive membership of the spiritual elite. Adult baptism was the rite through which one entered the elite. As infant baptism was one of only two sacraments that the other Protestant groups retained, all of the major Protestant groups rejected the Anabaptists. Anabaptists also tended to mysticism and claimed to be commanded by direct communications from God. Many rejected entirely the authority of the state and refused to pay taxes, abide by the decisions of the courts, or perform military service. Both Protestants and Catholics regarded Anabaptists with horror and persecuted them for heresy. The largest groups of Anabaptists, the Moravian Brethren, were eventually driven to the eastern edges of Europe, to Bohemia and Hungary. Smaller pockets of Anabaptists—the Mennonites, for example—settled in the Low Countries.

V.   The Catholic Reformation

A.   Introduction

The Protestant reform movement failed to eradicate Catholicism. Much of Europe remained resolutely Catholic. Within Catholicism, internal reform and renewed zeal for evangelism became evident.

B.   The Spiritual Revival

Late medieval Europe saw a renewed search for personal piety. This new piety led to the formation of communal societies of lay brethren, the most influential of which was the Brethren of the Common Life. Christian humanism also existed within Catholicism. These two movements defined the nature of early Catholic reform. Bishops took up the call for reform. Their concern was improving the quality of pastoral care provided by parish priests. New religious orders abounded in the sixteenth century. The Capuchins and Theatines are examples of attempts to return to principles of asceticism, poverty, and devotionalism. Women were also engaged in the reform of religious orders. Teresa of Avila led the reform of the Carmelite order. In Italy Angela Merici founded the Ursulines.

C.   Loyola's Pilgrimage

Ignatius Loyola began his life as a member of the Spanish aristocracy and as a soldier. A war injury led him to a religious life. During his convalescence, Loyola discovered the spiritual discipline necessary for Christian devotion. He recorded his methodology in *The Spiritual Exercises*. While seeking an education in France, Loyola gathered a small group of priests dedicated to the Spaniard's form of religious discipline. In 1540 the papacy recognized Loyola's brotherhood as the Society of Jesus, or Jesuits. The Jesuits became the principal arm of Catholic evangelism. Jesuits served as missionaries in the Orient and in the colonies and wilderness of the New World. The Jesuits continued Loyola's initial concepts of a disciplined society marshaled against the world's evils.

D.   The Counter-Reformation

The Jesuits reflected the Catholic Church's desire to confront Protestantism aggressively. Before an effective assault on Protestants could be waged, reforms within Catholicism were necessary. The papacy was generally resistant to further internal reform. Moreover, relationships among the major Catholic monarchs of Europe were complicated by the Italian Wars in which they were enemies. Conflicts within Catholicism delayed the calling of a general council of reform until 1545. The Council of Trent (1545–1563), dominated by Italian clergymen, recognized the demands of the papacy for a restatement of traditional orthodoxy. Reforms were limited to the most obvious abuses, such as indulgences. The early Catholic emphasis on pastoral care was recognized and reinforced. The council rejected Protestant theology outright.

E.   The Empire Strikes Back

Divisions within Protestantism and the fragmented nature of the Holy Roman Empire prevented the outbreak of warfare between Catholic and Protestant forces. Only after Luther's death did Charles V initiate an assault on Protestant territories in Saxony and Thuringia. Protestants then joined with the Catholic monarch of France and the Muslim Ottoman Empire in an alliance that drove Charles V to negotiation. In the Treaty of Augsburg of 1555, the emperor granted the princes of Germany the right to determine religious orthodoxy within their principalities.

TIMELINE

Insert the following events into the timeline. This should help you to compare important historical events chronologically.

Council of Trent begins
Loyola receives papal approval for Jesuits
Henry VIII divorces Catherine of Aragon

Zwingli expounds faith in formal disputation
Luther writes Ninety-five Theses
Calvin publishes *Institutes*

```
—— 1517

—— 1523

—— 1533

—— 1536

—— 1540

—— 1545
```

TERMS, PEOPLE, EVENTS

The following terms, people, and events are important to your understanding of the chapter. Define each one.

Johannes Gutenberg
Sir Thomas More
Johann Tetzel
Ninety-five Theses
Huldrych Zwingli
John Calvin
Henry VIII
Thomas Cranmer
Mary Tudor
Moravian Brethren
Jiménez de Cisneros
Saint Teresa of Avila
Society of Jesus

Christian humanism
Polyglot Bible
Frederick III the Wise
sola fide
Geneva
predestination
Catherine of Aragon
Thomas Cromwell
Thirty-nine Articles
Mennonites
Gian Matteo Giberti
Ursulines
The Spiritual Exercises

Desiderius Erasmus
In Praise of Folly
Martin Luther
sola scriptura
Wittenberg
Council of Trent
Anne Boleyn
Pilgrimage of Grace
Anabaptists
The Imitation of Christ
Catholic devotionalism
Ignatius of Loyola
Francis Xavier

MAP EXERCISE

The following exercise is intended to clarify the geophysical environment and the spatial relationships among the important objects and places mentioned in the chapter. Locate the following places on the map.

Wittenberg   Saxony   Geneva
Mainz   Zurich

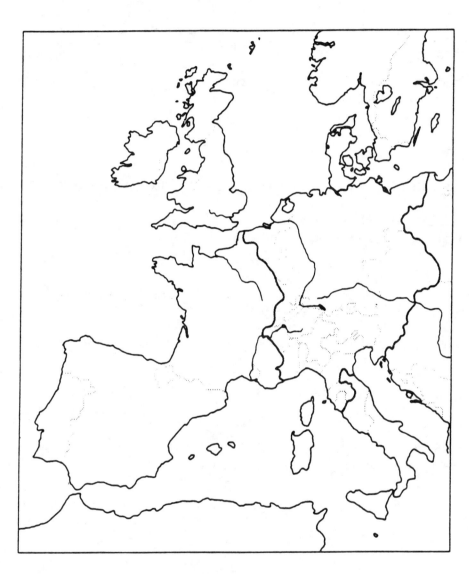

1. In what nation were the points of origin of the various Protestant beliefs—Lutheranism, Calvinism, Reformed religion, and Anabaptism? Given what you know about the political organization of that nation, why do you believe that religious rebellion occurred first in that area?

MAKING CONNECTIONS

The following questions are intended to emphasize important ideas within the chapter.

1. What was the impact of the print revolution?

2. Define Christian humanism. What did the Christian humanists attempt to accomplish in terms of reform?

3. What initiated the Lutheran reformation? What were the foundations of Luther's theology? How did Lutheranism spread throughout Europe? How were people attracted to it?

4. Compare and contrast Lutheranism and Calvinism.

5. Why did ecclesiastical reform begin in England? What was the nature of the Anglican church?

6. What was Anabaptism? Where and how did it spread?

7. What did the spiritual reawakening of Catholicism entail? What groups were founded as a result?

8. How did the Catholic Church respond to the Protestant rebellion? How effective was the Council of Trent? What changes were made in the Church?

PUTTING LARGER CONCEPTS TOGETHER

The following questions test your ability to summarize the major conclusions of the chapter.

1. In what way did the Protestant Reformation reflect the political configuration of Europe? What motives, other than religious, did people have for adopting a form of religion other than Catholicism?

2. How correct were the Catholics when they challenged the early Protestants with the statement "Schism breeds schism"? How homogeneous was the Protestant movement?

SELF-TEST OF FACTUAL INFORMATION

1. The primary difference between Christian humanism and Italian humanism was that

    a. the Italians were atheists.
    b. the Christian humanists rejected study of the classics.
    c. Italian humanists were more interested in secular subjects.
    d. Christian humanism developed a philosophy, the Italians did not.

2. The Polyglot Bible established what version of Scripture as superior to the Vulgate?

    a. Hebrew
    b. Spanish
    c. French
    d. Latin

3. One of the problems facing the Catholic Church in the sixteenth century was that

    a. in the wake of the Renaissance people were discarding faith as an irrational hangover.
    b. people wanted more of the Church than it could provide.
    c. increasing literacy rates contributed to the growth of the number of atheists.
    d. Erasmus wanted to start his own religion.

4. In 1517 Martin Luther was

    a. an ignorant peasant.
    b. a court advisor to Frederick III, the Wise.
    c. an Augustinian monk teaching at Wittenberg University.
    d. a lawyer laboring in the Mainz courts.

5. Which of the following was *not* a major tenet in Luther's religious views?

    a. justification by faith
    b. faith through the study of God's Word
    c. approaching God through good works
    d. the equality of all believers in God's eyes

6. How did the Lutheran reformation affect women?

    a. There was no impact on women.
    b. Elite women tended to reject Protestantism and call for its suppression.
    c. Luther's continued insistence on a celibate clergy offended women.
    d. The doctrine of equality of all believers put women on an equal spiritual footing.

7. In his concept of predestination, Calvin taught that

   a. all believers had the gift of faith before birth.
   b. some believers had the gift of faith, but good works remained necessary for God's pleasure.
   c. the pastors of each individual congregation could determine who would have the gift of faith.
   d. the gift of faith was given by God only to some and all peoples' salvation or damnation is decided before birth.

8. During what reign were the primary doctrinal and devotional changes made in the Anglican Church?

   a. Henry VIII
   b. Edward VI
   c. Mary Tudor
   d. Elizabeth I

9. The Council of Trent

   a. offered the olive branch of compromise to the Protestants.
   b. made no concessions to the Protestants.
   c. made significant doctrinal reforms in Catholic theology.
   d. punished Tetzel for his abuse of selling indulgences.

10. What work did Ignatius Loyola publish?

    a. *The Imitation of Christ*
    b. *In Praise of Folly*
    c. *The Soul's Journey to God*
    d. *The Spiritual Exercises*

Chapter 14

Europe at War, 1555–1648

OUTLINE

I.   The Massacre of the Innocents

War was a common feature of European society even before the mid-sixteenth century. After 1550, warfare spread throughout the European continent. Violence linked together dynastic ambition, social rebellion, and sectarian hatred.

II.   The Crises of the European States

A.   Introduction

One king and one faith was the organizing principle for the monarchies of western Europe. The Protestant Reformation destroyed the easy unanimity of political power and religious faith. As European populations were divided in religious belief, internal disruption of the state was inevitable. Only the total victory of Catholics or a single variety of Protestantism could restore the solidarity of the state.

B.   The French Wars of Religion

Because French monarchs suppressed earlier varieties of religious reform, Protestantism was exported to France from Calvin's Geneva. By 1560 Calvinism had gained a foothold in France, particularly within the provincial towns. At the same time, the death of the reigning French monarch, Henry II, left his fifteen-year-old son and his widowed queen, Catherine de Médicis, in control of the royal administration. The weakened central government permitted the creation of a powerful political faction within the French aristocracy. The Catholic Guise family allied itself with the royal family and dominated the offices of state and of the Catholic Church in France. The Guises were intent on the destruction of Protestant nobles who represented a possible opposition. Their situation became less secure when Francis II died, leaving his younger brother, Charles IX, on the throne. Sensing the weakness of the Guise position, Protestant nobles led by the Bourbon family and Henry of Navarre raised armies and initiated a civil war in 1562. Neither side was able to gain a decisive advantage. The Protestants were reduced to defending cities in their control, largely in southern France. Catherine de Médicis unsuccessfully sought a truce that would guarantee the position of her remaining sons. An attempted compromise that would permit Protestantism among the nobility was undone when the head of the Guise family was assassinated. A second diplomatic effort was initiated in 1570. Henry of Navarre was offered the hand of Charles IX's sister with the wedding to take place in Paris. The proposed marriage proved to be a deception intended to lure Protestant leaders to the capital city where they could be slaughtered by the Guise retainers. The result was the Saint Bartholomew's Day

Massacre of 1572. Many Protestants were murdered in the streets, but the leaders escaped.

C.   One King, Two Faiths

The collusion of Catherine de Médicis in the Saint Bartholomew's Day Massacre allowed Henry of Navarre and the Huguenots (as French Protestants were called) to launch an attack on the monarchy itself. Some moderate Catholic nobles, appalled by the bloodshed in Paris, joined forces with the Huguenots. Conservative Catholics responded by forming the Catholic League. The League, still led by the Guise family, was even willing to alter the monarchy in order to avoid any compromise with the Protestants. The monarchy seemed on the verge of losing its authority to one or another of the parties. King Henry III ordered the assassination of the leading members of the Guise family and attempted to gain a treaty with Henry Bourbon and the Huguenots. The sad chronicle of political duplicity and murder reached its climax with the assassination of the king in 1589. The sole successor to the Valois throne was Henry Bourbon, king of Navarre and leader of the Huguenots. In order to make his claim acceptable, Henry IV renounced Protestantism and converted to Catholicism. Such a diplomatic conversion, however much it may have lacked in sincerity, allowed Henry to claim the support of the papacy and the moderate Catholics. Resistance to the monarchy collapsed. In 1589, Henry made the settlement as palatable as possible to the Huguenots by offering them limited toleration. The passions of religious division were not entirely calmed. An assassin murdered Henry IV in 1610.

D.   The World of Philip II

Spain under King Philip II was the most powerful nation in sixteenth-century Europe. His domain included Naples, Milan, the Netherlands, Portugal, and the colonies of the New World. Philip exercised a personal supervision over the affairs of his far-flung empire. Philip also presented himself as the protector of Catholicism and the scourge of Protestantism. Briefly married to Mary I, the Catholic queen of England, Philip hoped to retain England for Catholicism and as a Spanish ally. When Mary's successor, Elizabeth I, returned to the Protestant Anglican Church, Philip amassed a great armada to attempt an amphibious assault on England. The Armada was largely destroyed by weather and English ships in 1588.

E.   The Burgundian Inheritance

Philip's attempts to secure Catholic orthodoxy were particularly problematic in the Low Countries. The source of conflict was the rapid dissemination of Calvinism in the tolerant communities of the Low Countries and Philip's attempts to enforce the decrees of the Council of Trent. Both the local nobility and the town governments refused to implement the repressive measures of Philip's decrees.

F.   The Revolt of the Netherlands

A Calvinist assault on Catholic churches initiated violence. The Spanish government viewed the iconoclasm as open rebellion with the tacit approval of the local nobility. Philip dispatched an army under the command of the Duke of Alba to restore order and orthodoxy. Alba imposed a martial reign of terror. Protestant nobles and suspected revolutionaries were executed under the authority of the military tribunal, the Council of Blood. In the short term, brutal suppression of Protestantism was effective. The Protestant movement was supported by those who resented not only the presence of the Spanish army, but also the taxation required to support it. In 1572 a full-scale civil war between the

Spanish regents and Protestants ensued. Prince William of Orange led the Protestant movement, centered in the provinces of Holland and Zeeland. Alba's failure led to his removal from command, but undisciplined Spanish troops continued to loot the towns of the southern Low Countries. Brussels, Ghent, and Antwerp were sacked. The unrestrained violence of the Spanish army so discredited the Spanish presence in the Netherlands that Philip II granted autonomy in the Pacification of Ghent of 1576. What remained was a divided territory. Five provinces agreed to remain Catholic and recognize the authority of the Spanish monarch. The remainder declared their independence. Despite continual military efforts to bring the northern provinces back under the aegis of the Spanish government, Holland remained independent. The war was economically ruinous for all involved.

III.   The Struggles in Eastern Europe

A.   Introduction

Dynastic struggles more than religious discord troubled the states of eastern Europe.

B.   Kings and Diets in Poland

In 1572 Sigismund II, the last of the Jagiellons, died. In the absence of an heir, the Polish nobility elected the royal successors from available nobility elsewhere in Europe. In return for aristocratic favor, successful candidates conceded constitutional and religious rights to the nobility. The Polish Diet, a representative body of nobles, gained many powers, including the right to establish a policy of religious toleration. Throughout the sixteenth century, Poland-Lithuania remained militarily and economically strong. In 1587 Sigismund III, also heir to the Swedish crown, was elected king in Poland-Lithuania. While he accepted the principle of religious toleration, he acted to strengthen Roman Catholicism. Poland resolutely refused to support Sigismund's attempts to enforce his claims in Sweden.

C.   Muscovy's Time of Troubles

Following the death of Ivan IV the Terrible, the principality of Muscovy began to disintegrate. With no capable heir and without the support of the Muscovite aristocracy, the central government disintegrated. After 1601 numerous claimants to the throne battled with one another for superiority in the period referred to as the Time of Troubles. Poland-Lithuania sought to capitalize on the problems within Muscovy and to retake lands lost in the past. The Polish monarch, Sigismund III, turned from abortive campaigns in Sweden to an assault on Muscovy. When a plan to support one of the Muscovite claimants to the throne failed, Sigismund took Moscow and had himself proclaimed tsar in 1610. Sigismund III's reign as tsar of Muscovy was short-lived. In 1613 the Russian boyars united against a foreign enemy and elevated Michael Romanov to the office of tsar. Romanov was able to arrange for a peace with Poland in exchange for territorial concessions.

D.   The Rise of Sweden

Sweden had been part of a Danish confederation until the rebellion of Gustav I Vasa in 1523. Thereafter Gustav ruled an independent Sweden in tandem with the Swedish aristocracy, who voiced their concerns through the Rad. Under Gustav, Sweden launched an aggressive foreign policy aimed at dominating the Baltic Sea regions. With the failure of the Teutonic Knights in Livonia, Sweden gained a foothold in Livonia on the Gulf of Finland through the fortification of sea ports on the

Livonian coast. The Livonian outposts gained Sweden substantial control over Baltic trade with Muscovy. Sweden was soon drawn into conflict with Poland and Denmark over control of Baltic trade. Sigismund III of Poland had a claim to the Swedish throne. The Swedish aristocracy rebuffed Sigismund's attempts to secure both crowns and elected Charles IX in 1604. The election provoked conflict with Poland, but gave the Swedes an opportunity to extend their control over Livonia. Their primary objective was the port of Riga, a major center of eastern trade. Although the Swedish navy enjoyed success, the Poles destroyed their land forces and forced a Swedish retreat. Only the Polish invasion of Muscovy occasioned by the Time of Troubles saved the Swedes from loss of Livonia. Just as the Swedes were involved in the conflict with Poland, the king of Denmark, Christian IV, attempted to renew Danish claims to sovereignty in Sweden. In order to avoid a war on two fronts, the Swedes gave away nearly all of their trade advantages in the Baltic to Denmark in 1613. King Gustavus Adolphus (1611–1632) succeeded Charles IX in the midst of the northern conflicts. With the invaluable support of the English and the Dutch—both of whom had trade interests in the Baltic—Gustavus Adolphus led the Swedes to military victory in the north. Renewed war with Poland ended the claims of Sigismund III to the Swedish throne and garnered the port of Riga. Muscovy surrendered its territories in the Gulf of Finland in return for Swedish support against the Poles. By 1619, Sweden was firmly in control of the eastern Baltic.

IV.   The Thirty Years' War, 1618–1648

A.   Introduction

European warfare between 1555 and 1648 combined the worst aspects of dynastic and religious conflict. Long years of dynastic struggle for hegemony and internal religious strife came to a head in the Thirty Years' War.

B.   Bohemia Revolts

The Holy Roman Empire remained fragmented religiously and politically. The Peace of Augsburg guaranteed to each prince the right to determine the religious orthodoxy of his principality. The empire remained, as it had since the Golden Bull of 1356, decentralized. At the beginning of the seventeenth century, the head of the empire, the Habsburg emperor, presided over the eastern states of Austria, Bohemia, and Hungary. To secure the succession for his Catholic nephew, Emperor Mathias granted the monarchy of Bohemia to Ferdinand Habsburg. A staunch Catholic, Ferdinand rapidly alienated the Protestant majority of his new kingdom. A group of Protestant nobles rebelled against Ferdinand's government and physically threw two officials out of a window in the royal palace. This assault, the Defenestration of Prague, signaled the start of Protestant revolts throughout the Habsburg domains. Spain immediately joined their imperial Habsburg relatives to put down the Bohemian rebellion. In 1619 Ferdinand succeeded Mathias as Holy Roman Emperor. At the same moment, Frederick of the Palatinate, a Protestant prince, accepted the vacant Bohemian throne. War between Ferdinand and Frederick was inevitable. The first stage of the conflict that became known as the Thirty Years' War was a complete victory for the Catholic allies over the Bohemian pretender. Ferdinand's forces conquered their adversaries at the Battle of White Mountain and sacked Bohemia, which was added once again to the Habsburg estates. The victory of the Catholic emperor caused Protestant princes to seek potential allies in case the ruler wished to press his advantage in the empire.

C.   The War Widens

To meet the Spanish and imperial Habsburg challenge, a group of Protestant allies—England, Holland, Denmark, and some German principalities—determined to carry on the conflict. In 1626 a Danish army invaded the empire. Under the command of Albrecht von Wallenstein, the imperial forces easily dispatched the Danish threat. By 1629 the Danes withdrew as leaders of the Protestant coalition. The emperor used his military superiority to reduce the influence of Protestantism within the borders of the Holy Roman Empire. Toleration for Calvinists was revoked, and all lands taken from the Catholic Church had to be returned. German Protestants had little choice but to unite in opposition to the emperor. In 1630 Gustavus Adolphus of Sweden assumed the leadership of the scattered Protestant alliance. Sweden's monarch hoped both to defend the northern tier of German Protestant principalities and simultaneously to protect Swedish interests in the Baltic. A wartime atrocity at the Protestant city of Magdeburg galvanized the Protestant opposition. Saxony and Brandenburg, previously hesitant to join the conflict, entered on the side of the Swedes. By 1631 the Protestant forces were able to seize the initiative and invade Catholic territories. The Palatinate was recaptured and Catholic Bavaria fell to the Protestant invaders. In the midst of his success, Gustavus Adolphus was killed at the battle of Lutzen.

D.   The Long Quest for Peace

With the king of Sweden's death, the theater of war changed from central Europe to the west. In 1621 the Spanish renewed their war with the independent provinces of Holland. Temporarily distracted by the early stages of the Thirty Years' War in the empire, the Spanish were unable to bring all of their military forces to bear on Holland. In the meantime, the naval superiority of the Dutch led to a series of Spanish embarrassments. The Dutch razed Spanish colonies and attacked the New World treasure fleets. In 1627 the expenses of warfare so strained the Spanish treasury that Philip III was forced to declare bankruptcy. Sensing the declining fortunes of the Habsburg powers, France declared war on Spain in 1635. The primary location of war between France and Spain was the Spanish Netherlands on the northern border of France. Neither side was able to gain a military advantage, but the effects of many years of warfare were harsher for the Spanish. The Dutch won another great victory at sea over the Spanish fleet in 1639. At the same time, the Portuguese rebelled in order to regain their independence. By 1640 all of the rulers and major figures involved at the outset of the Thirty Years' War had died. Those who succeeded them wanted nothing more than to end the endless rounds of warfare. Unfortunately, each of the combatants wanted to gain an advantage out of the peace negotiations. Only in 1648 was the Peace of Westphalia hammered out. It generally recognized Protestant and French gains at the expense of the Habsburgs. Spain agreed irrevocably to Dutch statehood. Sweden gained its superiority over the Baltic ports of northern Germany. France gained territories in the Lower Palatinate that closed the Spanish military highway to the Low Countries. Within the empire, the terms of the Peace of Augsburg were restored and explicitly extended to include Calvinists. The powers of the emperor were further weakened in favor of the princes.

TIMELINE

Insert the following events into the timeline. This should help you to compare important historical events chronologically.

Defenestration of Prague
Peace of Westphalia
Calvinists begin revolt of Netherlands

Twelve Years' Truce
Saint Bartholomew's Day Massacre
Edict of Nantes

—	1566
—	1572
—	1598
—	1609
—	1618
—	1648

TERMS, PEOPLE, EVENTS

The following terms, people, and events are important to your understanding of the chapter. Define each one.

Catherine de Médicis
Henry Bourbon
Saint Bartholomew's Day
Catholic League
revolt of the Netherlands
"Spanish fury"
Time of Troubles
Charles IX
Gustavus Adolphus
Albrecht von Wallenstein

Guise family
Huguenots
Edict of Nantes
Philip II of Spain
Duke of Alba
Poland-Lithuania
Michael Romanov
Christian IV
Defenestration of Prague
battle of Lutzen

Francis II
politiques
Duc de Condé
Spanish Armada
William of Orange
Sigismund III
Gustav I Vasa
Thirty Years' War
Christian IV of Denmark
Peace of Westphalia

MAP EXERCISE

The following exercise is intended to clarify the geophysical environment and the spatial relationships among the important objects and places mentioned in the chapter. Locate the following places on the map.

Locate the various states belonging to Philip II.
Mark the Protestant states of Europe with a "P," Catholic states with a "C."

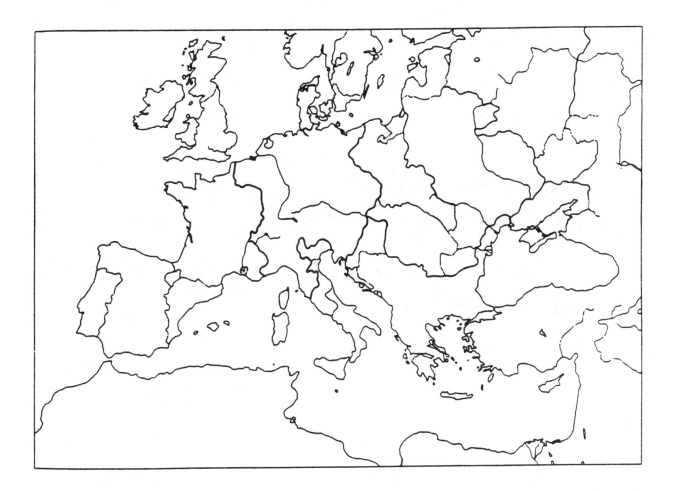

1. What country was most threatened by the Habsburg Empire of Philip II? How does that help to explain the nature of European history in the sixteenth and seventeenth centuries?

2. Does religion explain the alliance systems of the Thirty Years' War?

MAKING CONNECTIONS

The following questions are intended to emphasize important ideas within the chapter.

1. Why did the Reformation lead to internal violence in European states? What states were involved in internal religious wars?

2. What states engaged in the struggle for dominance around the Baltic? What state emerged as the most successful?

3. What were the causes of the Thirty Years' War? How did the emperor's success at the battle of the White Mountain lead to a wider conflict?

4. How did the final stages of the Thirty Years' War involve new nations in the conflict?

5. What was the solution to European violence in the Treaty of Westphalia?

PUTTING LARGER CONCEPTS TOGETHER

The following questions test your ability to summarize the major conclusions of the chapter.

1. In both France and the Spanish empire, religious wars involved a Catholic state against a Protestant rebellion. How were the two revolutions different? In what ways were they similar? Consider, for example, the results of each.

2. Was the Thirty Years' War dynastic or religious in nature? Explain the motives of each of the combatants for their involvement.

SELF-TEST OF FACTUAL INFORMATION

1. The power behind the throne during the French wars of religion was

   a. Lorenzo de Medici.
   b. Philip II of Spain.
   c. Mary, Queen of Scots.
   d. Catherine de Médicis.

2. What family dominated the French offices of state under Francis II?

   a. the Medicis
   b. the Guises
   c. the Bourbons
   d. the Habsburgs

3. In the Saint Bartholomew's Day Massacre

   a. Henry Bourbon was assassinated.
   b. the Guises were assassinated.
   c. there was indiscriminate slaughter of Protestants, but most of the Huguenot leaders escaped.
   d. there was indiscriminate slaughter of Catholics, but most of the Catholic leaders escaped.

4. The *politiques* were Catholics who

   a. formed the Catholic League.
   b. desired a practical settlement of the civil wars.
   c. plotted the assassination of Henry Bourbon.
   d. joined the royal government in opposition to the Huguenots.

5. Henry Bourbon justified his conversion to Catholicism after succeeding to the French throne by saying,

   a. "I've been a Lutheran and a Calvinist. Why not a Catholic?"
   b. "God will forgive me."
   c. "Paris is worth a mass."
   d. "The kingdom of France is greater than any religion."

6. In 1609 Spain and the Netherlands concluded the

   a. Peace of Augsburg.
   b. Peace of Westphalia.
   c. Twelve Years' Truce.
   d. Defenestration of Prague.

7. Which of the following was initially a French Huguenot?

    a. Henry Guise
    b. Henry Bourbon of Navarre
    c. Catherine de Médicis
    d. Henry II

8. The Pacification of Ghent of 1576 included all of the following terms *except*

    a. local autonomy in taxation.
    b. the immediate withdrawal of all Spanish troops.
    c. the central role of the States-General in legislation.
    d. the independence of the northern states of Holland and Zeeland.

9. The selection of a monarch for what German kingdom precipitated the Thirty Years' War?

    a. Bavaria
    b. Bohemia
    c. the Palatinate
    d. Hanover

10. Which of the following was *not* a term included in the Treaty of Westphalia?

    a. Sweden gained further territories in the Baltic.
    b. Spain recognized the independence of Holland.
    c. The Peace of Augsburg was abandoned as the definition of religion within the Holy Roman Empire.
    d. The powers of the Holy Roman Emperor were weakened with respect to other German states.

Chapter 15

The Experiences of Life in Early Modern Europe, 1500–1650

OUTLINE

I.   Haymaking

Sixteenth-century life remained largely rural and agricultural. Men and women toiled in fields along with their neighbors. Housing was still constructed of wood and thatch. It was more spacious and comfortable than medieval domestic housing, but not by much. The parish church, the grandest building in an agricultural village, still dominated the rural landscape.

II. Economic Life

A.   Introduction

Sixteenth-century society varied from one region to another and from one social class to another. There was no typical European. The long-delayed population recovery from the Black Death transformed European society.

B.   Rural Life

Villages varied in size from one hundred families in western Europe to twenty families in eastern Europe. Peasants made up the majority of the European population and were recruited by the state and aristocracy for labor and military service. Much of the income from the village went to the payment of taxes, rents, and tithes. Agricultural productivity was precarious. Crops barely sufficed to supply the agricultural village. Winter, crop diseases, and changes in weather were likely to result in food shortages. Peasant housing was crude, often consisting of a single long hall with a fireplace for heat and a single window to the outside world. Housing was shared during bad weather with animals. Peasant personal property was limited—a chest, a table, a bedstead, some pots and utensils. Peasant life was controlled by the agricultural seasons. In northern Europe, the primary organization of land was the three-field rotation in which winter wheat, spring crops, and fallow were alternated. Wheat was the commercial crop, while the peasants consumed bread made of the less valuable rye and barley. In the Mediterranean climatic region, a two-field rotation remained the rule. Grain crops were supplemented by Mediterranean luxury products—olives and grapes. In mountainous areas throughout Europe, animal husbandry was practiced. Sheep were the most common domesticated animal. In wooded areas, pigs were kept. The most common draught animal was the ox, bred in great numbers in eastern Europe. Most land was owned by the state, the Church, or the aristocracy. In western Europe, peasant land ownership was more common than in eastern Europe. In contrast, labor service as a condition of land tenure was much more common in the east than in the west. In general, western European peasants had greater social and economic mobility than their eastern counterparts. Within any village, there were variations in wealth and social status among the peasantry.

C.   Town Life

If nature defined agricultural life, city life was an environment of human invention. Guilds continued to regulate the conditions of labor, as they did in the Middle Ages. Towns were more market-oriented than rural villages. Labor was exchanged for a greater variety of goods than in the countryside, although abject poverty remained a problem. Urban occupations were varied. In smaller towns the market in food items dominated exchange. Women often were prevalent in these trades. Smaller towns tended to be semi-agricultural with fields farmed by urban citizens. In larger towns, there was a greater variety of occupations. Wholesale merchants controlled the major crafts and markets, while individual households supplied unskilled labor. Crafts in larger towns were concentrated in specific quarters rather than spread randomly throughout the urban space. Even in larger towns, some tasks—midwifery, prostitution, and wet-nursing—were reserved for women. Most citizens survived by periodic employment as unskilled laborers. Domestic service was a common occupation. Towns survived on the basis of a regular supply of foodstuffs. To insure it, some towns owned agricultural lands. Grain was often stored in municipal warehouses, and urban councils strictly controlled food prices.

D.   Economic Change

The catalyst for economic change was population growth throughout Europe. Cities tended to increase in population more rapidly than rural regions. Initially the population increase spurred economic growth. With more available labor, lands abandoned during the Black Death were brought back into cultivation. Agricultural productivity increased. Greater supplies of foodstuffs supported larger urban populations, which in turn increased the supply of manufactured goods. Increased population pressure eventually forced extension of the agricultural system to lands less fertile and to areas formerly reserved for animal husbandry. In some cases, actual colonization of the wilderness took place to meet the insatiable demand for foodstuffs. By the middle of the sixteenth century, the economic situation deteriorated. Crafts in the towns reached their labor saturation point. Guilds began to limit new admissions, and wages generally fell as the supply of workers increased. The decline in wages was more traumatic because of contemporary inflation. The so-called Price Revolution was the result of two events: the importation of vast quantities of bullion discovered in the New World and the widespread practice of debasing coinage. The impact of the Price Revolution was enormous. Grain prices climbed faster than those for manufactured goods, putting tremendous pressure on urban councils to hold the line on food prices. Those who held long-term contracts for rents suffered, while those who received payment in kind profited. Peasants who depended on the value of their labor for supplemental income were made destitute. In peasant communities, the social distinctions between those who owned land and those who did not became more pronounced. In eastern Europe, where peasant land ownership was uncommon, the aristocracy used the situation to further bind the peasantry in servitude. In the west, landless vagrants with little hope of employment wandered from village to village.

III.   Social Life

A.   Introduction

Sixteenth-century social life was stratified. People identified themselves with a particular group, rather than as individuals. The rapid economic change of the sixteenth century challenged the traditional social organization of Europe.

B.   Social Constructs

Sixteenth-century society consisted of an interlocking set of hierarchies—within the nobility, crafts, urban government, even the household. Status largely determined one's position in the hierarchy. Social conventions dictating courtesy between various groups, manners of dress, and titles all were symbols of status. All things and people had a specific place in the hierarchy, a concept represented by the Great Chain of Being and reinforced in the political metaphor of the Body Politic. Status, according to the social theories of the day, was static.

C.   Social Structure

European society was supposedly divided into two status groups—nobles and commoners. Nobility implied certain privileges, notably the title granted and the right to bear a coat of arms. The nobility also possessed political rights. Members of the nobility were, by their status, eligible for high office in the state and customarily summoned to representative institutions. Nobles also held economic advantages over commoners. In most cases, the nobility paid no taxes, a significant exclusion. In return for their favored status, nobles were expected to serve as military commanders. By the sixteenth century, the professionalization of warfare limited the military role of the nobility, but accentuated their administrative function. Between the nobility and the commoners, a new group without clear status was emerging. In function, it differed little from the nobility, although it did not enjoy either title or privilege. Urban elites tended to be members of this group. Some of the wealthiest and most powerful townsmen successfully transferred themselves to the lower levels of the nobility. In the countryside, those who were able to obtain greater quantities of land in the course of the sixteenth century clearly separated themselves from the class of agricultural laborers from which they sprang. This group is often referred to as the gentry. Even among the commoners, there were clear hierarchies of status usually related in rural villages to ownership of land or freedom from labor service. In towns status was connected to citizenship.

D.   Social Change

The expansion of the state and the creation of new wealth unrelated to noble status placed stress on the European social system. In the long run, the hierarchies of social status were inevitably changed. On the positive side, noble titles increased as the population growth required more people eligible to govern. Employment in the state offered opportunities for wealth and advancement. For some, the Price Revolution proved to be a windfall. On the negative side, the population explosion dramatically increased the numbers of destitute. The burden of care of the poor fell on local communities. When the ability of local charities to care for the poor was exhausted, the state intervened. In many cases, the state was more concerned with the problem of controlling vagrancy than in alleviating the plight of the poor. Imprisonment and corporal punishments were imposed on vagrants.

E.   Peasant Revolts

Changes in social organization led to conflict between the orders. Peasant revolts, although often moderate in purpose and well organized, were brutally suppressed. Many peasant revolts were in response to changes in the agricultural system imposed by surges and recessions in the economy. Protection of woodlands and enclosure of open fields for commercial agriculture provoked strong peasant responses. Both had deleterious effects on the small landholder. Peasant revolts broke out in Hungary in 1514, England in 1549, Germany in 1525. The German revolt, although disowned by Martin Luther, combined an assault on both the secular and ecclesiastical nobility. Peasants objected to changes taking place in agricultural villages and demanded freedom from serfdom. Their desire for stability contradicted the volatile economy of the sixteenth century.

IV.   Private Life

A.   Introduction

Despite the revolutionary nature of sixteenth-century political and economic developments, there was continuity in private life. Strongest ties remained to family and local community.

B.   The Family

Family was at the foundation of private life. In western Europe, the nuclear family was most common. In eastern Europe, the nuclear family was also prevalent, although extended households were more common than in the west. Kinship ties bound the family to other groups within rural communities. The family also stressed the relationship between past generations and the present. Among the nobility this tendency was more pronounced in the forms of inheritance and coats of arms, but it also existed in the transfer of land from one peasant generation to the next.   The individual household was also an economic unit, with all members contributing their labor to its welfare. Households were subject to the authority of the adult parents. The husband was titular head, but children and servants were responsible to both husband and wife. Despite population growth, the size of the typical family remained small. Infant mortality and relatively late age of marriage for women depressed the birth rate. Women endured many pregnancies during their lives. The economic role of women within the household was varied. Wives prepared food, kept domestic animals, educated children and provided primary child care, made clothing, and cleaned. In towns women might add the tasks of selling goods and directing domestics. Men performed more public duties—the primary agricultural tasks, the construction of farm equipment, performance of owed labor services, and participation in the political life of the village. Marriage was the normal social condition for both men and women.

C.   Communities

Households existed within a community structure, either rural or urban. Communities were organized by the secular and ecclesiastical lords. Rural lords established conditions of labor and land usage. The village church was both a spiritual and social center, a focal point for holidays and celebrations. Communities expressed their social solidarity by ceremonial activities in which all members of the village participated. In rural villages, priests led residents in annual perambulations of the lands. In towns, ceremonial processions were more formal and reflected the greater social stratification of urban life. Weddings were significant ceremonies for the entire community. Marriages bound families—and often wealth—together. They marked the admission of a new household to the community. Because property and community approval were involved, weddings were public affairs. Other festivals were associated with the passage of stages of the agricultural cycle. Festivals released community members from labor and presented opportunities to resolve community squabbles. Festivals also offered the chance for the social hierarchy of the community to be placed on public display.

D.   Popular Beliefs

Despite the print revolution, most Europeans remained illiterate. The common man's sense of the world around him was individual and experiential, not scientific. Not surprisingly, sixteenth-century society was imbued with the magical. Magical solutions abounded for medical problems, changes in the weather, disastrous harvests, and for prediction of future events. Use of magical powers for evil was considered witchcraft. Consultation with the black powers of evil spirits and the devil, himself, brought the repressive powers of the churches into play. Prosecutions for witchcraft became common in the sixteenth century. Women were most often the objects of prosecutions for witchcraft.

TERMS, PEOPLE, EVENTS

The following terms, people, and events are important to your understanding of the chapter. Define each one.

manorial rents	parish tithes	wooden chest
black bread	*robot*	guilds
specialization of labor	domestic service	Price Revolution
Gdansk	hierarchy	status
Great Chain of Being	Body Politic	*Book of Gold*
Esch	villein	"deserving poor"
sturdy beggars	enclosure	Ket's Rebellion
Peasants' War	public sphere	domestic sphere
annual perambulation	processions	Carnival
rites of May	skimmingtons	witchcraft

MAKING CONNECTIONS

The following questions are intended to emphasize important ideas within the chapter.

1. What was the peasant household like? What was the nature of peasant agriculture? What was the relationship of the peasantry to the soil? How did this relationship differ between east and west?

2. How did town life differ from that of the agricultural village? How was the town linked to the village?

3. What were the two basic changes in the economy of sixteenth-century Europe? What were the causes of the Price Revolution? What was its effect on village and town?

4. What was the strucutre of sixteenth-century European society? On what metaphors was it based?

5. How did the family and the community serve to maintain social stability?

PUTTING LARGER CONCEPTS TOGETHER

The following questions test your ability to summarize the major conclusions of the chapter.

1. What were the elements of sixteenth-century life that mandated stability? How did these constructs and institutions limit change?

2. What were the elements of change in sixteenth-century Europe? Was change or stability more critical to sixteenth-century life?

SELF-TEST OF FACTUAL INFORMATION

1. Which of the following would *not* be typical in an average rural village?

    a. Farming was still a communal activity.
    b. The Protestant Reformation reduced the significance of the village church.
    c. Both men and women labored in the fields.
    d. Villages showed signs of population growth.

2. What distinguished Mediterranean agriculture from that of northern Europe?

    a. a two-field rotation
    b. no domesticated animals
    c. absence of cereal crops
    d. absence of the vine and the grape

3. Labor service was

    a. dying out as a relationship between lord and peasant all over Europe.
    b. more common in western Europe than in the east.
    c. enforced by the European states to control vagrancy.
    d. more common in eastern Europe than in the west.

4. Which of the following was *not* a change in the agricultural system brought about by the population increase?

    a. Poorer lands were abandoned as more intensive effort was placed on fertile areas.
    b. Animal flocks diminished as less land was available for animal husbandry.
    c. Colonization of previously uninhabited areas took place.
    d. Woodlands were diminished.

5. Which of the following did *not* occur during the Price Revolution?

    a. Grain prices rose faster than those of manufactured goods.
    b. Landlords with long-term rents suffered.
    c. Landlords who received payment in kind benefited.
    d. Wages continued to rise throughout the century.

6. Which of the following was *not* a challenge to traditional social organization in the sixteenth century?

    a. the rise to wealth and prominence of new social groups
    b. rising numbers of rural and urban poor
    c. migration of large numbers of people to New World colonies
    d. transformation of landholding patterns in villages

7. Which of the following was *not* a factor causing changes at the top of the social scale?

   a. new wealth created by the Price Revolution
   b. opportunities for advancement in state service
   c. the need for more governors due to the population increase
   d. the tendency to pass titles on to all male children

8. Magical practices

   a. were restricted to the poor and illiterate.
   b. were limited to circles of witches and sorcerers.
   c. appealed to people at all levels of society.
   d. were virtually unknown in the sixteenth century.

9. The most common targets of investigation for magical practices were

   a. the insane.
   b. children.
   c. men.
   d. women.

10. Which of the following community activities was a celebration of the community's dead?

   a. perambulation
   b. All Hallows' Eve
   c. Carnival
   d. rites of May

Chapter 16

The Royal State in the Seventeenth Century

OUTLINE

I.   Fit for a King

Versailles represented the power, prestige, and wealth of the state. Built at extraordinary expense, Versailles became the architectural persona of Louis XIV's absolutism. So intent was the monarch on creating a public image that the private accommodations were meager and uncomfortable. In the same fashion, the majesty of Louis XIV's France was a veneer over the poverty and unhappiness of some of his people.

II.   The Rise of the Royal State

A.   Introduction

Warfare at the outset of the seventeenth century was, itself, a cause for the development of a more centralized state.

B.   Divine Kings

In the seventeenth century monarchs became the personification of the power of the state. Palaces and capital cities magnified the public aura of kings. Portraiture was utilized to express royal majesty. Literature and history were subordinated to the glorification of monarchy. Royalty was elevated to the level of mythos. Political theory matched the arts. The divine right of kings held that God created the institution of monarchy and appointed kings as his representatives on earth to ensure good order. King James I actually wrote a treatise on the divine right of monarchs entitled *The True Law of Free Monarchies*. More surprisingly, the theory of rule through heavenly appointment was generally accepted outside the circle of monarchs. In order to properly exercise the powers ordained by God, a monarch had to act in the best interests of his people—rule through good laws, pursue peace and prosperity. Kings who failed to rule according to divine dictates—whatever they were perceived to be—risked God's wrath. Kings became synonymous with the public performance of the duties of state, and all monarchs were constrained to appear in front of their subjects.

C.   The Court and the Courtiers

In fact, the duties of government in the seventeenth century were larger in scope than one man or woman could possibly handle. Consequently, more state officers were required to manage the growing burden of government. As courts expanded, once independent aristocrats were co-opted into royal service. Royal councillors grew in wealth, prestige, and power as they gained the ability to create executive policy. The point of contact between monarch and royal council was often a personal favorite—either an officially appointed chief minister or simply a personal companion with more frequent access to the king or queen. Favorites were often shields for monarchs against public displeasure with royal policies. A number of men best represent the powers and dangers of becoming a royal favorite. In France the most powerful official of the royal government during the reign of Louis XIII was Cardinal Richelieu. During his early political career, Richelieu enjoyed the patronage of Marie de Médicis, mother of Louis XIII. As chief minister of France, the cardinal took over the most burdensome governmental duties of the monarch leaving Louis free to pursue less arduous pastimes. A brilliant manager of public affairs, Richelieu undertook the tasks of state centralization. His success earned him many powerful enemies, but he died in office in 1642. Count-Duke Olivares succeeded to his family's titles and fortunes. Rather unusually, Olivares also obtained a university education. Olivares' power was attributable to his position as personal favorite of Philip IV of Spain with immediate access to the monarch. Olivares, like his French rival Richelieu, was intent on the construction of a centralized monarchy. Unfortunately for him, the failure of his aggressive foreign policy led to his dismissal from office in 1643. James I elevated the Duke of Buckingham from the ranks of the commoners to the nobility of England. Buckingham's position as the royal favorite allowed him to gain influence within the royal government, particularly in the military. Buckingham survived the death of James I to become the royal favorite of Charles I. His continued role of influence and power within the royal court alienated many of the English nobility. When his foreign policy schemes failed, Parliament attempted to have him removed from the king's presence. The support of the monarch frustrated parliamentary attempts at impeachment, but a disgruntled naval officer assassinated Buckingham in 1628.

D.   The Drive to Centralize Government

Despite the attempts of monarchs and personal favorites to increase the power of the central government, powerful regional elements existed within all the states of western Europe. One of the primary means of achieving centralization over the regions was the creation of strong central legal systems. In France, the parlement (or central court) expanded in the seventeenth century. Royal justice was extended to the various districts of France, as the number of regional parlements increased. As courts grew, so did the influence of professional lawyers. Similarly in Spain, those with legal training entered the administration of the kingdom. In England the growth of regional courts outdistanced the development of the central court system. The monarchy delegated the responsibility for local court systems to members of the local elite who were named justices of the peace. Justices were required to maintain law and order in the countryside until the arrival of one of the judges of the central courts. In addition to the extension of legal systems, it was necessary for monarchs to appoint new officials to represent royal interests in the provinces. In France, the intendants began to replace the aristocratic provincial governors, who spent much of their time in Paris rather than in the countryside. Intendants were not normally part of the regional aristocracy in the districts they governed. As a result, they were more responsive to the needs of the central administration. The local officials in England were called Lords Lieutenant. England, alone among European states, was without a standing national army. The function of the Lords Lieutenant was to raise, equip, and train a local militia on royal demand. Needless to say, English armies were not the most proficient in Europe. In Spain regionalism was more problematic than in France or England. Catalonia, in particular, insisted on the maintenance of its traditional separatism and regional rights. Olivares was unable to overcome the centrifugal tendencies of the Spanish regions. Both Portugal and Catalonia eventually rebelled against the central government.

156

E.   The Taxing Demands of War

War and the taxation it required was the engine that drove state consolidation. Taxation also produced opposition to the royal administration from all levels of European society. Armies increased in size, artillery and gunpowder were new and necessary expenses, and food and fodder rose in cost. Military action caused real economic hardship in terms of damages for those in the path of marauding armies, increases in food prices, and raised taxes. Exclusion of the nobility from taxation in the western states caused the burden of taxation to fall on those least able to afford it. States resorted to all sorts of stratagems to increase their income. England's constitution required the monarch to receive the approval of Parliament before initiating new taxes. Despite governmental shortfalls, Parliament proved hesitant to approve taxation. Most royal revenue was derived from customs duties on luxury imports. In the 1630s, Charles I attempted to impose an ancient duty that required ports to supply ships in times of naval crisis on all English towns, even those far from the water. The gentry generally refused to accept the royal innovation and took the royal government to court in a constitutional challenge of the king's right to tax.

III.   The Crises of the Royal State

A.   Introduction

The expansion of the state occurred at the expense of other corporate entities—the Church, towns, and aristocracy. Often immune from taxation, the corporate bodies nevertheless relied on their own ability to mulct the peasantry. More efficient and intrusive legal systems disrupted the traditional patterns of local authority. At the same time, population pressure on the agricultural system led to failures in the food supply. Responses were violent. At first resistance was on a local level. By the 1640s, the focus of resistance was the state itself and the concept of divine monarchy.

B.   The Need to Resist

Disease, crop failure, and the effects of war on noncombatants caused European population to decline in the seventeenth century. Until 1750 all segments of the economy stagnated. Poor weather contributed to setbacks in agriculture that were most devastating to the peasantry. In France the increase of the *taille,* the tax on property, led to disorder and rebellion. Most revolts were directed against local tax collectors and strictly limited in objective. In England, local resistance was aimed at halting the progress of enclosure of open fields. In the Spanish kingdom of Naples, the shortage of food in the city of Palermo led to rebellion. When the disorder forced the government to abolish the tax on foods, similar revolts broke out in the city of Naples. Success for rebels was short-lived. The royal government suppressed both movements.

C.   The Right to Resist

Peasant rebellions, generally opposed by local elites, could not succeed in the face of national armies. Only when the aristocracy joined in the cause of rebellion could the state be threatened. The right to rebel developed in curious combination with the theories of divine monarchy. As kings were God's representatives on earth, it became not only possible but necessary to dethrone tyrants—those who did not rule according to the divine strictures of upholding justice and piety. The duty of rebellion fell at first on lesser magistrates and members of the elite, but later was extended to all members of the Body Politic. Attempts to murder James I of England failed, but in 1610 Henry IV of France did fall

157

to an assassin. John Milton completed the theory of righteous rebellion by adding the concept of a contract between monarch and the governed. In *The Tenure of Kings and Magistrates*, Milton suggested that if kings failed in their contractual obligations to rule well, citizens could dissolve the contractual relationship between themselves and the ruler to reconstitute the state. The theoretical justification of rebellion was put into practice in the Spanish dominions in 1640. In that year both Portugal and Catalonia rejected the authority of the Spanish monarch. Portugal, only recently added to Spanish possessions, achieved its goal of independence. Catalonia, long a part of unified Spain, represented a more serious threat to Olivares' attempts at state consolidation. The Catalan elite embraced what was initially a peasants' rebellion and declared the contractual relationship between themselves and Philip IV dissolved. Despite French intervention, the Catalan revolt failed. Like Spain, the French government was virtually bankrupt by 1640. When Louis XIV succeeded to the throne as a minor, the government under the direction of Anne of Austria and Cardinal Mazarin chose to raise taxes on officeholders and the aristocracy. When the Parlement of Paris refused to register the new taxes, the confrontation between royal government and the regional elite was inevitable. The Fronde, as the aristocratic rebellion was called, threatened an appeal to Spanish intervention in order to force concessions from Mazarin. Unwilling to agree on a program of constitutional reform and unable to control the deterioration of order in the cities of France, the Fronde lost its popular mandate. The royal government was swiftly restored.

D.   The English Civil War

The most severe disruption of monarchical rule occurred in the least likely of countries, England. James I, the king of Scotland, succeeded Elizabeth without dissension in 1603. Initial resistance to the Crown arose over the elevation of Scottish favorites to English offices. In addition, the royal government was forced to operate without a sufficient tax base. Requests to Parliament for additional revenues produced parliamentary demands for reform. In 1628 Parliament issued the Petition of Right restating the traditional freedoms of the English elite. In response, Charles I chose not to call a Parliament between 1629 and 1640. Adding to the dissatisfaction with the royal government was unhappiness with the state church. Puritans demanded a more Calvinist form of religion, including the abolition of the episcopacy of the Anglican Church. James I and his successor Charles I both saw the bishops as part of the hierarchy of the state and refused reform on this issue. Both monarchs attempted to strengthen the authority of the bishops, not to reduce it. In Archbishop William Laud, the Anglican Church received a conservative head bent on a more formal liturgy in contradiction to the Puritans' demands for a more rigorous brand of Calvinism. When a new prayer book to which all churches were supposed to conform was introduced in Scotland in 1637, the Scottish nobility refused to allow its imposition. When Charles I tried to gain parliamentary taxes to support military suppression of the religious and political uprising in Scotland, it refused. The Long Parliament first met in 1640. Instead of granting fiscal support, the Parliament demanded constitutional reform and the removal of specific royal councillors. Archbishop Laud was imprisoned. Charles' chief political advisor, the earl of Strafford, was executed. When Charles' belated and clumsy attempt to arrest leading members of the Long Parliament failed, the king withdrew from his capital in 1642 to raise a royal army. Parliament also called for military support to confront the king's military. The king was able to gain the support of much of the English aristocracy. Parliament enjoyed the support of those who sought religious reform. By 1645 parliamentary forces gained a military advantage. Charles I, actually a prisoner of Parliament, refused to cooperate with his conquerors. In the face of royal intransigence, the uneasy coalition of opponents of the Crown began to disintegrate. Religious moderates and radicals created new political alignments.

E.   The English Revolution

Religious radicals were concentrated in the parliamentary army, which in 1647 became the central force in prosecuting the rebellion against royal authority. The army and its commanders easily defeated remaining royalist forces. When it appeared that moderates in Parliament might seek a new agreement with Charles I, the army invaded London and purged moderates from the representative body. The remaining radicals in Parliament, called the Rump, brought the king to trial and convicted him of tyranny. Charles' execution in 1649 led to the abolition of monarchy and the establishment of a commonwealth under the remainder of the lower house of Parliament. The Rump was unable to create a viable constitution. When the Rump's failure became obvious, Oliver Cromwell, commander of the army, expelled the remnants of the Long Parliament. Cromwell adopted the title of Lord Protector under a new constitution called the Instrument of Government of 1653. Cromwell refused the offer of a crown and attempted to govern through Parliament and the Council of State. After Cromwell's death, there was no viable candidate to succeed him as Protector. In 1659 army commanders called for the restoration of the monarchy. After lengthy negotiations, Charles II, son of Charles I, returned to England in 1660. The restored monarchy was forced to recognize the authority of Parliament and the limitations of royal power. Both the state religion and the limited authority of the crown were challenged in the reign of James II. When the king attempted to openly support Catholicism, virtually all elements of English authority rejected the monarchy. In 1688, with the encouragement of many in England, William of Orange and his wife, Mary Stuart, invaded. With virtually no support, James II had little choice but to become an exile. Parliament recognized William and Mary as joint monarchs to govern under an agreement called the Declaration of Rights. The so-called Glorious Revolution of 1688 produced a new political theorist, John Locke. In *Two Treatises on Civil Government*, Locke proposed a social contract that existed between rulers and their subjects. In the contract, the governed gave up some of their unlimited natural rights to the ruler in order to secure greater liberty and freedom from violence. Monarchs who acted arbitrarily or failed to protect the rights of their subjects could be deposed.

IV.   The Zenith of the Royal State

A.   Introduction

In the aftermath of the mid-century rebellions, the search for political stability became a primary goal of monarchs and regional political elites. Royal reforms of administrative policy were balanced by a greater willingness on the part of the regional elites to cooperate with the central government. While England, Holland, and Sweden developed balanced constitutions that limited the role of the monarchy, elsewhere the rule of government was royal absolutism.

B.   The Nature of Absolute Monarchy

Most countries were unwilling to grant the degree of political freedom necessary for the operation of a balanced constitution. More common was the development of absolute monarchy along the lines developed by Thomas Hobbes. In *Leviathan*, Hobbes theorized that humans in a "state of nature" engaged in constant warfare. To avoid such internecine strife, men gave up their rights to rulers who undertook the restoration of law and order, the only guarantee of individual rights. Absolutism involved reverence for the person of the monarch as the symbol of the state, the consequent diminution of other elites within the state, personal management of the government by the ruler, decline of influence of representative bodies, and growth of the military. Absolutism remained more theoretical than practical. It depended on a capable ruler, the absence of religious diversity, and the will of the governed to support the government.

C.   Absolutism in the East

One of the most successful absolute monarchies existed in the newly created state of Brandenburg-Prussia. Frederick William took over the region in the tragic aftermath of the Thirty Years' War. Without a tax base, with a population devastated by the religious wars, and with the aristocracy (the Junkers) virtually independent, Frederick William had little foundation for absolutism. He first instituted an excise tax, then built a strong national army controlled through a national war department. Russia, too, established absolutism in the wake of military reform. Tsar Peter I determined to adopt western European patterns of political organization and modeled his national army after that of Brandenburg-Prussia. After numerous failures, the military reforms resulted in the defeat of Sweden at the battle of Poltava in 1709. Peter also compelled the emulation of western European patterns of dress and appearance. In public administration, Peter divided Russia into regional districts controlled by royally-appointed officers and created departments of state with charge over specific tasks.

D.   The Origins of French Absolutism

Cardinal Richelieu was the initial architect of absolutism in France. Richelieu attempted to neutralize what he perceived as the three greatest threats to the French state: the position of the Huguenots in positions of power, the independence of the aristocracy, and the freedom of action enjoyed by regional governors. Richelieu brought the nobility under the rule of law, appointed intendants to undercut the authority of regional governors, and revoked the privileges of self-government jealously guarded by the Huguenots. Richelieu's policies of centralization brought on the Fronde.

E.   Louis le Grand

Richelieu's foundation for absolutism was advanced during the reign of Louis XIV. During the king's minority, Cardinal Mazarin tutored the young monarch in statecraft. The cleric brought the Fronde to a close and continued the war against Spain. In 1661, Louis personally assumed the tasks of government without a chief minister. He was served, however, by powerful assistants. Jean-Baptiste Colbert directed the financial aspects of France and led the country to solvency through greater efficiency. The Marquis de Louvois was responsible for the development of the military. He enacted reforms in logistical organization, the command structure, and recruitment. Louis intentionally excluded the old nobility of the sword from public administration. Ministers managed departments of state through small councils of professional bureaucrats. The connection between the central government and the provinces remained the intendant, an office that became even more important under Louis XIV. Louis played the part of state symbol better than any other monarch. Versailles became the facade for statecraft. The French aristocracy was emasculated through required service at the royal palace where they were reduced to enacting complex rituals of etiquette. The appearance of Versailles established Louis' court as the most majestic in Europe. French culture was widely emulated elsewhere in the capitals of kings. Absolutism depended on the capability of the king. Louis, though able to create a magnificent stage on which absolutism was played, bankrupted France through an aggressive foreign policy. The king also renewed the persecution of Protestants, creating an embittered minority committed to the destruction of French absolutism.

TIMELINE

Insert the following events into the timeline. This should help you to compare important historical events chronologically.

end of the Fronde	Russians win battle of Poltava
execution of Charles I	Glorious Revolution in England
revolution in Palermo	Catalan rebellion

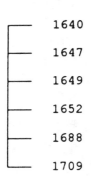

    1640

    1647

    1649

    1652

    1688

    1709

TERMS, PEOPLE, EVENTS

The following terms, people, and events are important to your understanding of the chapter. Define each one.

Ben Jonson	William Shakespeare	James I of England
True Law of Free Monarchies	Jean Bodin	favorite
Cardinal Richelieu	Count-Duke Olivares	Duke of Buckingham
letrados	justice of the peace	assizes
intendants	Lords Lieutenant	Ship Money
Nu-pieds	Philippe Duplessis-Mornay	John Milton
Catalan rebellion	French Fronde	Cardinal Mazarin
Petition of Right	Puritans	Archbishop William Laud
Long Parliament	Oliver Cromwell	Rump Parliament
Instrument of Government	Lord Protector	Glorious Revolution
Declaration of Rights	Toleration Act	John Locke
contract theory	absolutism	Thomas Hobbes
Frederick William	Junker	Peter I the Great
battle of Poltava	*raison d'état*	Jean-Baptiste Colbert
Marquis de Louvois	Versailles	Louis XIV of France

MAP EXERCISE

The following exercise is intended to clarify the geophysical environment and the spatial relationships among the important objects and places mentioned in the chapter. Locate the following places on the map.

Locate the states with limited or constitutional monarchies.
Locate the states with more absolute forms of government.

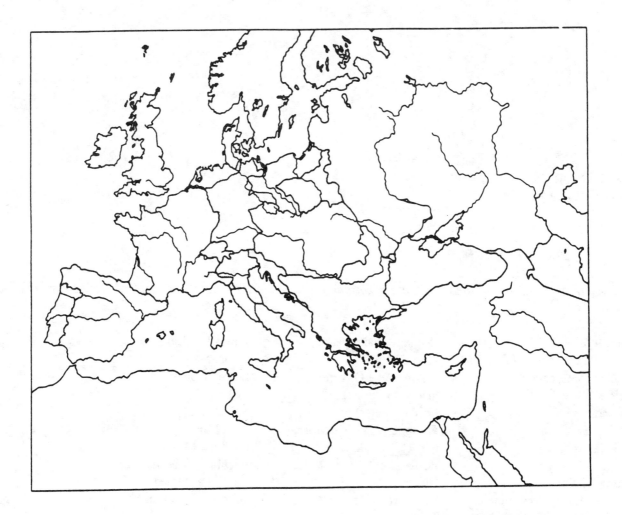

1. What geographic element characterizes those states with limited or consitutional monarchies? What impact would dependence on the sea have on the nature of government? [Consider, for example, the role of merchants.]

2. What form of government was more typical of the previously decentralized portions of central Europe? What explanation could account for this fact?

MAKING CONNECTIONS

The following questions are intended to emphasize important ideas within the chapter.

1. What was the "divine right of kings"? To what extent was it accepted in Europe?

2. How did divine right theory affect the structure of government? What was the role of favorites?

3. How did warfare affect monarchies?

4. What were the origins of the royal crises of the seventeenth century? What theories were elaborated that permitted resistance to the monarchy?

5. What factors account for the rebellions in England? What was their result? How did the Glorious Revolution lead to the development of Locke's social contract?

6. What was the nature of royal absolutism?

7. What was absolutism in eastern Europe initially based on?

8. What was the basis for French absolutism? How did Louis XIV complete the creation of absolute government? How successful was it?

PUTTING LARGER CONCEPTS TOGETHER

The following questions test your ability to summarize the major conclusions of the chapter.

1. In what ways did the concept of statehood change in Europe during the seventeenth century? What were the elements of the new state as it emerged under Louis XIV? Was the concept of royal absolutism accepted everywhere in Europe?

2. How did the European concept of the state differ from that of China or India? What are the similarities and differences in the concept of administration, for example? Would the Chinese have found European absolutism progressive or crude?

SELF-TEST OF FACTUAL INFORMATION

1. Which of the following did *not* result from the increasing significance of warfare in the seventeenth century?

   a. the loss of royal authority
   b. the growth of the size of royal armies
   c. the increased importance of defense to governments' functions
   d. the erosion of the traditional privileges of the towns

2. All of the following were artists associated with royal portraiture *except*

   a. Diego Velázquez.
   b. Peter Paul Rubens.
   c. Ben Jonson.
   d. Anthony Van Dyck.

3. The local county courts of England were referred to as

   a. Chancery.
   b. Common Pleas.
   c. King's Bench.
   d. assizes.

4. Which of the following statements concerning royal taxation in the seventeenth century is most accurate?

   a. England was able to escape the cycle of increased military activity and raised taxes.
   b. Most taxes were equitably distributed among all ranks of European society.
   c. In Spain and France much of the wealth of the nations was beyond the reach of traditional royal taxation.
   d. Most regimes were successful in reforming national systems of taxation.

5. Which of the following was *not* a cause of increased public dissatisfaction with royal government in the seventeenth century?

   a. increased taxation
   b. the absence of local officials
   c. bad harvests
   d. social and economic regulations

6. The aristocratic rebellion in France against the regency government of Cardinal Mazarin and Anne of Austria was called the

   a. Fronde.
   b. Catalan rebellion.
   c. Sicilian Vespers.
   d. Jacquerie.

7. Which of the following did *not* result from the English Civil War?

   a. Parliament became a permanent part of civil government and had to be managed rather than ignored.
   b. Religious toleration became the rule.
   c. Royal power over taxation was curtailed.
   d. Absolute monarchy became constitutional monarchy.

8. Who was responsible for the development of the contract theory of government as it developed in England after 1688?

   a. James II
   b. John Locke
   c. Thomas Hobbes
   d. Oliver Cromwell

9. Which of the following states did *not* develop royal absolutism?

   a. Sweden
   b. Prussia
   c. France
   d. Russia

10. Which of the following was *not* considered by Richelieu to be a threat to the establishment of absolutism in France?

   a. the fact that Huguenots shared the state
   b. the independent power of the provincial officials
   c. the long tradition of aristocratic independence from royal authority
   d. the unwillingness of Louis XIV to engage in personal government

Answers to Chapter Self-Tests of Factual Information

Chapter 1

1. a	6. a
2. c	7. c
3. a	8. c
4. b	9. a
5. d	10. b

Chapter 5

1. b	6. d
2. a	7. c
3. d	8. a
4. b	9. c
5. c	10. b

Chapter 9

1. c	6. c
2. c	7. c
3. a	8. a
4. c	9. b
5. d	10. a

Chapter 13

1. c	6. d
2. a	7. d
3. b	8. b
4. c	9. b
5. c	10. d

Chapter 2

1. c	6. b
2. d	7. b
3. b	8. a
4. c	9. d
5. d	10. d

Chapter 6

1. a	6. b
2. a	7. a
3. a	8. c
4. b	9. b
5. d	10. b

Chapter 10

1. b	6. c
2. c	7. c
3. b	8. c
4. d	9. d
5. d	10. d

Chapter 14

1. d	6. c
2. b	7. b
3. c	8. d
4. b	9. b
5. c	10. c

Chapter 3

1. d	6. a
2. b	7. c
3. b	8. c
4. b	9. c
5. d	10. d

Chapter 7

1. d	6. a
2. a	7. d
3. c	8. c
4. a	9. b
5. b	10. c

Chapter 11

1. d	6. a
2. a	7. b
3. d	8. d
4. b	9. d
5. c	10. b

Chapter 15

1. b	6. c
2. a	7. d
3. d	8. c
4. a	9. d
5. d	10. b

Chapter 4

1. b	6. b
2. a	7. c
3. a	8. c
4. d	9. c
5. d	10. d

Chapter 8

1. a	6. b
2. a	7. d
3. a	8. a
4. d	9. d
5. c	10. b

Chapter 12

1. a	6. c
2. b	7. b
3. c	8. d
4. d	9. a
5. d	10. d

Chapter 16

1. a	6. a
2. c	7. b
3. d	8. b
4. c	9. a
5. b	10. d